Economics
and Ethics

J. Philip Wogaman

Economics and Ethics

A CHRISTIAN INQUIRY

FORTRESS PRESS Philadelphia

Portions of chapter 3 appeared originally in "Theological Perspective on Economics" in *Morality of the Market: Religions and Economic Perspectives* © 1985 by The Fraser Institute, Vancouver, B.C., and are used by permission.

Excerpt from "Choruses from 'The Rock'" in COLLECTED POEMS 1909–1962 by T. S. Eliot, Copyright 1936 by Harcourt Brace Jovanovich, Inc.; Copyright © 1963, 1964 by T. S. Eliot. Copyright by Faber & Faber, London. Reprinted by permission.

Library of Congress Cataloging-in-Publication Data

Wogaman, J. Philip.
  Economics and ethics.

  Includes index.
  1. Economics—Moral and ethical aspects.
  2. Economics—Religious aspects—Christianity.
  3. Laissez-faire—Moral and ethical aspects.
  4. Capitalism—Religious aspects—Christianity.
  I. Title.
  HB72.W633   1986   261.8'5   85-45478
  ISBN 0-8006-1904-8

2097I85   Printed in the United States of America   1–1904

In Memory of
John W. Gattis VI

Contents

Preface

Economics touches all aspects of life. That is easy enough for most of us to see when our own pocketbook is involved, though we have greater difficulty grasping the interconnections between economic realities and other aspects of human society. Most people care about what happens to society, and some care passionately. But the relationship between our dreams and visions for the common life and the hard realities of economics often remains obscure.

This book is offered as a contribution to greater understanding of the connections between economic reality and social purpose. It is based on the belief that both cannot be understood apart from an ethical frame of reference. Economic process cannot be trusted to take care of itself, and it is far too important to turn over to professionals alone. In recent years there has been an intellectual and political onslaught against the broad use of government as an instrument of society in economic life. This return to the laissez-faire assumptions of an earlier era threatens once again to remove economics from purposeful debate and decision-making by the political community. Its effect is to divorce whole spheres of life from such debate and decision-making: education, health and welfare, conservation, labor relations, social inequalities, global economic relationships. The radical reassertion of laissez-faire in intellectual and political circles may have helped clarify many issues. But it is also fraught with danger, and it badly needs to be corrected.

Not least of the problems with laissez-faire economics is the loss of connection between material problems and the deeper moral and spiritual values of humankind. When material things and relationships are regarded as self-sufficient, they are too easily cut adrift from the values that give direction to the human venture. The result is a trivialization of economic life, distortion of human relationships, and fragmentation of spirit. Our life as economic beings is divorced from our true humanity, and both are diminished. While this book was being written, the Roman Catholic bishops of the United States released the first draft of their pastoral letter on economics. That impressive book-length document quickly claimed the serious attention of thinking Americans because it endeavored to reassert the moral dimension of economics. The draft pastoral has been misunderstood by many critics, usually when they have failed to note the bishops' distinction between their basic theological values and their specific diagnosis of particular economic issues. I think the bishops were clear enough about this; but the critics' difficulties may betray lack of familiarity with the relationships of values to facts and of facts to problems and solutions.

Anticipating similar problems here, may I note that the present book also deals with facts and values on different levels. My own value orientation is that of a Christian ethicist. Moral values are here ultimately grounded in Christian faith as I understand it. That should be particularly clear in the theological explorations of chapter 3. Those values are not, however, the exclusive possession of Christians. From time to time the moral analysis will proceed more inclusively, recognizing that non-Christians accept many of the same values while validating them in somewhat different ways. At the same time, the discussion will occasionally strike the reader as proceeding simply on a pragmatic plane. But lest there be misunderstanding of that, it should be remembered that pragmatism always presupposes a deeper value frame of reference. What is "practical" necessarily depends in part on what we hope to accomplish; and what we hope to accomplish is, in turn, an expression of our values. I have sought to clarify that point in chapter 1, particularly in the section dealing with "problems." The relationships among facts, values, and theology challenge creative thought and action by all of us. I shall be amply served if this volume challenges others to think more deeply about these relationships, even where the conclusions of other people differ from mine.

This book, my third dealing with issues of economics and ethics, has benefited from the contributions of more people than I can hope to acknowledge. Over the past few years I have had the privilege of engaging in many consultations on economics and ethics, including university and seminary lectureships, colloquia sponsored by research centers in the United States, Canada, and England, lectures and discussions in church settings in several parts of the United States, and the many discussions with my own students and colleagues at Wesley Theological Seminary and the Churches Center for Theology and Public Policy in Washington, D.C. I am particularly grateful to the Hinksey Center, Oxford, England, for specific stimulation to write on the theme of this book and for two delightful seminars under that center's auspices at Oxford in the summers of 1983 and 1985. The Fraser Institute of Vancouver, B.C., has kindly permitted me to use substantial material in chapter 3 from a paper originally produced for a conference under its auspices in 1982. The manuscript has benefited from critical reading by Mark Gibbs, an Anglican priest-scholar (who originally conceived the project), by Max Johns, a U.S. government economist and active Lutheran layman, and by Davis Perkins of Fortress Press. None of these good people is to be blamed for remaining errors of fact or judgment, but the book is surely better for their assistance. Virginia Hamner, faculty secretary at Wesley Theological Seminary, has again placed me in her debt for very competent secretarial services.

My wife, Carolyn, has supported this project in very important ways, not least in the reminder that the household is a microcosm of the larger economy, just as the family is the best clue to the meaning of universal community.

J. Philip Wogaman
Wesley Theological Seminary
Washington, D.C.

CHAPTER ONE

Economic Problems and Human Values

A few years ago I found myself locked in friendly argument with a group of economists, philosophers, and Christian ethicists at a conference on economics and ethics. For several days we debated the fine points of how to relate economic policies to the central values of Hebrew-Christian religious traditions. The philosophers and ethicists among us emphasized the centrality of basic religious values in arriving at economic policy decisions. The economists were equally insistent on the importance of technical economics. No doubt both "sides" had useful things to say for such an occasion.[1]

By midpoint in the conference a famous economist who was participating became weary of all the religious talk. Speaking with exasperation to a religious journalist and me during a coffee break, he said, "I challenge the two of you to come up with even one moral or religious value that we do not already hold in common." Lurking behind that seemingly fair-minded inquiry was a hidden assumption that was not lost on us. If we all hold the important values in common, then values themselves do not need to be examined. And if values do not need to be examined, policy questions can safely be turned over to the economists for purely technical solutions. If we already agree on the "ends" we all want, then only the "means" need be considered. And since economists are supposed to be the experts on the "means" questions, the rest of us can be excused from further participation in discussions of economic policy. That fact would not in itself settle all the important issues, since experts do not always agree on technical questions—a point clearly underscored in recent economic debate. But noneconomists could at least be relegated to the sidelines.

My journalist friend and I were not sure we should concede the economist's point and become spectators for the rest of the conference. There really did seem to be important value disagreements among the conference

1

participants; and in the case of the famous economist with whom we were in debate, it appeared to us that his values were much more individualistic than ours. Moreover, he clearly did not share our theological orientation. But in replying to him, we decided to make a simpler point. Even if we were all in agreement about the values to be sought by reasonable and moral people (which we may or may not have been), it is also very important to know which values should be given preference in the event of conflicts among the values. That is to say, the relative priority we give to different values is in itself also a very important value judgment. In this case, the economist might agree that community and mutual love are good, but whenever such values are in conflict with individual freedom they must be subordinated. Our own view on that kind of conflict was, we thought, a more refined one. It was at least very different from his. We gave higher priority to some values than he did; he gave higher priority to others.

The Importance of Economic Life

We can all agree that economic life is very important. Broadly speaking, it is the production and distribution of scarce goods. Scarce goods are things that people want (whether or not they need them). To say that economic goods are ''scarce'' is simply to acknowledge that the supply is limited. Effort must often be put forth to create the supply or make it accessible. There may not be enough to go around among those who want some of it.[2] Some things, like the air we breathe, are normally so abundant that we do not think of them as economic goods—although recent experience with air pollution is a good reminder that even the most abundant goods can become ''economic'' under some circumstances, with substantial effort being required to ensure that the quantity and quality continue to be adequate to supply the wants of people. Almost anything imaginable can be a ''scarce good'' under some conditions.

Nonmaterial things are also considered scarce goods. An idea, a poem or other work of art, a trademark, an ''option'' (to buy, to build, to mine)—the list is potentially endless—can require a good deal of effort and can become the basis for intense competition. It is said that 90 percent of law is concerned with property rights. I have made no independent effort to confirm that statistic, but I think it would be even more interesting to survey the many different forms that ''property'' takes. For wherever ''property'' exists and is protected by law, there is a ''scarce good.'' Much economic life is concerned about intangible goods that can, however, be limited either naturally or artificially.

Economic goods also include services rendered. The ministrations of physicians, the work of teachers, the performances of concert artists and professional athletes, the work of salespersons, and a host of others are not tangible objects, but they are goods in limited supply and sought by others. In the advanced stages of the Industrial Revolution, less and less effort has to go into producing the absolutely necessary goods (like food) and more and more can be devoted to services that enrich life. To make the point statistically, traditional agrarian societies typically devote more than 90 percent of their available labor resources to farming, leaving only 10 percent or less for manufacturing and services. By 1900 the U.S. economy had advanced to the point where 50 percent of the labor force was able to grow and harvest the food supplies needed by the rest. Today fewer than 3 percent grow the food supplies for the entire country and for an expanding export market. A similar process is discernible in relation to manufacturing where, with increasing automation and a computer revolution, fewer and fewer people are needed for the traditional "blue collar" industrial jobs and more and more people can be employed in "services." But whether the work done is farming, manufacturing, or services, it involves making or doing things that are needed or at least wanted and are in limited supply.

Both production and distribution are included in the definition of economic life: the process of making or developing or distributing goods and services and the system of allocating those goods and services. The fact that goods and services are scarce means that some way has to be found to decide who gets what. And so the whole intricate design of monetary exchange, accompanied by no small amount of conflict and controversy, has evolved as central to economic life.

These are the most rudimentary things that can be said about economic life, but it is clear that economics is of critical importance to the whole human enterprise. It involves our access to goods and services without which we would perish, along with most of the other things needed to enrich and ennoble—as well as degrade—humanity. It is inconceivable that humankind, placed on this limited planet as it is, could ever be able to ignore economics altogether—although there might come some happy time in the future when abundance would so overtake scarcity as to make competition for scarce goods less a preoccupation.[3] Plainly we are not there yet; and even if that day of abundance should arrive we would doubtless find that much of life still must revolve around what to do with and about economic goods and services. Economics is important.

What about economists? Paraphrasing Clausewitz (who said that war is too important to leave to the generals), we might remark that economics is too important to the human enterprise to leave in the hands of economists

alone. Many economists would agree. But in the friendly debate with the
economist referred to in the beginning of this chapter, that was really the
issue at stake. Should economic decisions and policies be turned over to
the technical experts? Plainly economists have a very significant contribution to make. It is their professional responsibility to help us understand
the distributional systems and problems and to see how these affect processes and problems of production. Much of this is very technical. Economists, like other professionals, can only trivialize their field when they
use technical jargon to protect their status and decision-making power vis-
à-vis nonprofessionals. The problem is not with technical terminology
as such. Most fields of learning develop such terminology for the sake
of greater precision of speech and greater efficiency of communication
among experts. The term "Phillips Curve," for instance, has little meaning to most noneconomists. But among professional economists the term
is shorthand for noting the belief that the rate of inflation is correlated
with the employment rate: the less unemployment there is the higher the
rate of inflation may be expected to be. Based on some observation of
fact, this relationship was worked out mathematically by the economist A.
W. Phillips in a fairly elegant "model." The term "Phillips Curve" and
mathematical modeling facilitate communication among those who are
trained in the discipline, and the actual work on which the term and the
modeling rest is clearly relevant to important social problems and policies—such as the problem of how to combat inflation or unemployment.

But the use of the terminology and mathematical modeling can be a way
of obscuring, not clarifying, reality. By treating the "Phillips Curve" as a
generally accepted economic dogma and by underscoring its authority by
emphasizing the precision of mathematical modeling, we may lead the lay
public and policy-makers to believe that there is an exact relationship
between inflation and full employment. Many people have in fact been led
so to believe. In American debates over unemployment and inflation it is
not unusual to hear it said that it is inflationary to have the unemployment
rate dip below, say, 6 percent. The "Phillips Curve" almost implies that if
we only knew enough we could chart exactly how much unemployment is
needed to keep inflation at this or that precise level. But a false precision
can be the worst enemy of clarity. Much historical evidence can be cited to
show the weakness of the "Phillips Curve" as overall theory, for there
have certainly been periods in the United States, Japan, and other countries where low inflation rates accompanied nearly full employment.
(Conversely, during much of the 1970s several Western countries had both
high inflation and high unemployment.) The problem is that there are
other things at work, particularly the cultural values and expectations of
people, which are not subject to precise measurement or predictability.

In an illuminating discussion of econometrics, Lester C. Thurow points out that "the random component in economic events is much larger relative to the deterministic component than most confident economists thought earlier."[4] Since unforeseen economic events (shocks) and the unpredictable aspects of human nature cannot be built into the econometric model with precision, the model cannot be a "good predictor." And, he adds, "without good predictions it becomes difficult to operate the economic controls—taxes, expenditures, money supplies, and interest rates—to obtain the economic results desired by the public." By implying a high degree of predictability to their models, economists can lead the public and policy-makers to mistrust other relevant forms of knowledge and insight, including intuitions derived from broad human experience.

But economists exercise their professional responsibility most seriously when they help clarify technical questions in such a way that nonprofessionals can participate along with them in the debate over the best economic policies to be pursued and in such a way that other valid sources of knowledge will be brought to the fore, not obscured. Above all, it is important for economists and lay public alike to remember that economic policies always involve nontechnical value judgments along with technical factors. A good technician helps clarify alternatives and limitations.

To illustrate this last point: in the discussions of welfare reform during the past quarter-century, well-meaning lay participants have sometimes urged that an income guarantee be provided all poor people at a level sufficient to bring them up to the poverty line, while also allowing them to keep additional earnings as an incentive. Economic technicians cannot settle the policy questions on the basis of their expertise alone, but those economists who have studied welfare questions carefully have helped clarify the actual cost to society of implementing such a wide-ranging program. There is a "break-even" point above which one would not be able to receive public assistance—and everybody currently receiving less income than the net sum anybody would be permitted to receive under the welfare-reform scheme (welfare grants plus supplementary grants) would become eligible for some form of aid. Many people currently receiving more than poverty-level wages might become eligible. Technical clarification of such relationships is a proper and valuable contribution by economists.[5]

But is it really true that economic policies also involve nontechnical value judgments?

The Contribution of Ethics

To answer that we have to understand the place of ethics in economic life. Ethics is often presented and understood too narrowly. Many people think of ethics only as a faintly distasteful catalog of do's and don'ts. It is certainly true that every society has moral rules to govern behavior, and the analysis of such standards is part of the work of ethics. But much more is involved than that. Ethics is finally based on conceptions of good and what is required to actualize good in human existence. The written and unwritten moral codes attempt to spell out the things people have to do or avoid doing if their lives are to contribute to good and not evil.

But much more is involved than moral rules (indeed, sometimes moral rules obstruct the good as much as they serve it). Ethics can help us understand the good and clarify the things that can be done in the real world to enhance its possibilities. In that sense, ethics is concerned about ends (the goods we seek) and means to ends (the steps required to achieve the ends). Ethics can also help us see the relationship between the ultimate source of good, which H. Richard Niebuhr called the "center of value," and the lesser goods or values that gain their meaning from that ultimate source or center.[6] Since economic life involves a host of such "lesser goods," ethics can best serve economics by clarifying how these economic values are related to the ultimate good.

This point can be clarified by recalling the philosophical distinction between intrinsic and instrumental values.[7] An intrinsic value is something that is good in and for itself. It requires no further justification. An instrumental value is something that is good because it contributes to the fulfillment of an intrinsic value—it is an "instrument" helping us gain something that is simply good in itself. Most of us would say, for instance, that a friendship is an intrinsic value. Friends help each other in an instrumental way, but a real friendship is not primarily to be used; it is something to be enjoyed and appreciated in and of itself. Food, clothing, shelter, transportation, medicine, and many other things are mostly useful because they help us gain other things. Music can be understood to be an intrinsic value, but a stereo recorder is valued principally because it gives us access to music—not because the stereo is good in itself. Political power is good because it can be used for the advancement of social good or justice; justice, on the other hand, is good in and of itself. Life is distorted when intrinsic goods are treated as though they were merely instrumental or when instrumental goods are invested with ultimate significance. That is a very important point to bear in mind as we come to address the relationship between social priorities and economic realities. For economics generally has to do with instrumental and not intrinsic values, and yet we are constantly invited to reverse the order. We are asked to treat human relationships and God-given talents as, primarily, ways of making more money—and we are implored to regard the acquisition of particular mate-

rial objects, like automobiles or items of clothing or housing, as essential
to our very humanity. Joining a church primarily for the sake of making
good business contacts illustrates one form of this reversal; measuring the
success of our lives by our cash income is another. Intrinsic goods are
degraded when turned into merely instrumental ways of getting something
else; instrumental goods are idols or false gods when treated as though
they were intrinsic.

Not that instrumental values are unimportant. Some intrinsic goods
simply cannot be gained without the right instruments. What, after all, is
friendship among people who have no food or protection from the elements and disease? What is great art in a setting of acute malnutrition? In
fact, what is a piano concerto without somebody making pianos and orchestral instruments to play it with? Instrumental values can be absolutely
vital to the realization of intrinsic values, so they are to be taken seriously.
But they are means to ends, not ends in themselves.

Many people, when they think of ethics, also tend to see this in purely
individualistic terms. There is a sense in which the moral life is radically
personal, for it does have to do with our basic attitudes and decisions and
the actions we choose to take or not to take. Some ethicists prefer to think
of the moral life almost entirely in terms of the development of character,
the cultivation of virtues, mature growth as a moral being.[8] And who
could deny the importance of that? But the moral life is also profoundly
social, both in the origin and cultivation of moral values themselves and in
the actions, policies, and institutions developed to realize them. One re-
members the theme of Reinhold Niebuhr's classic, *Moral Man and Immoral Society,* that seemingly moral individuals (who manifest all the
traditional virtues of character and loving disposition) can act socially in
such a way that evil triumphs and injustice prevails. Doubtless the relationship between the individual and social dimensions of morality is more
subtle than usually understood and each is inextricably tied to the other.
But my point is that we cannot be serious about the moral life if we forget
about the social context of the good. That, too, has important implications
for economic life which we shall have to pursue later. In the main we shall
be discussing public policy questions involving the overall direction to be
given to economic life. But it remains a very important issue how much
latitude and encouragement should be given for primarily individual economic endeavor and reward.

If the root of economic policy questions is the clarification of values,
does that mean that ethicists (rather than economists) should be turned to
for the right answers? Tempting as it might be for an ethicist to say yes to
that, it must also be said that the moral life is far too important to leave to

the ethicists. In fact everybody is involved in the moral life: in judging and deciding and acting. Ethicists can help clarify (or sometimes obscure) the value issues, just as economists can help identify (or confuse) the factual dimensions of economic life. But ethicists and economists alike need to be humbler about their contributions. Both are servants, not masters, of the process. Nobody's expertise is up to the task of telling society what values it should live by. We are all involved in dealing with the great questions together.

"Problems" and "Solutions"

But still, there may be some who wonder whether the value dimension is being given too much emphasis here. There is, after all, quite a tradition of treating economic policy questions less elaborately as problems to be solved. The problem-solving approach is especially important in the economic background of the Anglo-Saxon countries, with the Japanese more recently teaching the rest of the world a lesson or two. In that tradition of healthy pragmatism, one does not start with ideologies into which the economic world is made to fit. One starts with the problem at hand and addresses it with an eye toward actually solving it—perhaps later taking note of the theoretical implications of what one has done, in good scientific fashion.

I do not wish to denigrate economic pragmatism. The world could surely stand more of it as it wrestles with truly overwhelming problems. But at the same time I think we should look a bit more closely at what a "problem" *is*. Apart from purely theoretical problems that tease the imagination and challenge intellectual skill, we normally think of problems as difficulties to be overcome or new possibilities to be realized. That is, we are really concerned about values to be gained, or protected, or enhanced in a setting where those values are being resisted.

My house is on fire. That is a "problem" for me because I value the house and want to preserve it. So I do several things to solve the problem: use the fire extinguisher, call the fire department, take valuable things out of the house so they won't be destroyed by heat, smoke, and water. Or, my stomach is acting up. I do not know the source of the pain, but it is depriving me of the value of feeling good and it may even be life-threatening if I do not deal with it. So I go to the physician for diagnosis and treatment. He or she takes on the problem along with me, and together we try to define it more accurately and solve it. Or, I have a falling out with a valued friend. The friendship is an important value to me, so the broken relationship is a problem I must solve if I possibly can. So I summon whatever human relations skills I possess and maybe enlist the services of others to help repair the damage. Or, I get lost while on a long trek in the wilderness. Night is coming on, it is growing colder, the skies threaten rain. I know I will not be able to find my way out of the wilderness before morning, so I set about to find some way to shelter myself from the cold and a possible storm, thereby gaining the value of comfort and possibly preserving the value of health or even life itself. Clearly, in all such instances, the very definition of the "problem" to be solved entails an understanding of values that are at stake.

But then, is it not true that we can all agree on the values at stake, and therefore on the problems to be solved? Who could disagree about the desirability of shelter from the storm (or of saving one's house from fire or of dealing with physical pain)? True enough, we agree that these and many such problems involve commonly accepted values, and the step from this to economic problems of all kinds should be fairly obvious. But what is a problem to one person may not be a problem to somebody else. Indeed, one person's "problem" may even be somebody else's solution! For instance, the apartheid system of racial discrimination in South Africa is (rightly) viewed as a terribly serious problem by millions of black, colored, and Indian people who together make up a large majority of the population of that country. But at the same time many, perhaps most, of the white people do not think of it as a problem at all.[9] For them, the only problem is to keep the black, colored, and Indian people in a subservient status. For such whites, therefore, apartheid is not a problem; it is a *solution*. Thus, the value question is perceived almost exactly in reverse of the way it is understood by the oppressed majority.

Such an opposition of problems and solutions is not characteristic of every human situation. Sometimes communities recognize common problems and address them in a united way—for example, in confronting the effects of a great natural disaster or in constructing some needed new institution or building. But the reversal of problems and solutions is more typical of economics than one might suppose. To be sure, there is a sense in which most people stand to gain from the overall material progress of a society so that the problem of improving the goods and services for society as a whole is one that we largely share (bearing in mind that there may be many differences of opinion as to which goods and services ought to be produced). But much of economic life presents conflict, not community of interest. Remember that a very large aspect of economics is the *distribution* of *scarce* goods. What goes to one person or group may not be available for distribution to others. So what is a solution to the first will be a continuing problem to the others. This is not at all unusual in the normal course of economic life; it is rather typical.

Let us consider by way of illustration two of the substantial economic problems the world has confronted in the 1970s and 1980s.

First, the dramatic rise in world petroleum prices. This caused genuine hardship in many developed countries, with painful increases in the costs of fuel for automobiles, heating, public utilities, and industry. Most people experienced some lowering of their standard of living as a result, either directly or indirectly. Governments scrambled for ways to meet the crisis, sometimes with ingeniously contrived problem-solving. The United States, for example, explored the development of alternative sources of energy, such as liquefaction of coal, further development of solar- and wind-powered devices, and even the conversion of garbage into energy. Many people sought ways of conserving energy, including purchase of more energy-efficient automobiles and the construction of better mass transit systems. All of this might seem to suggest that everybody was recognizing and responding to a genuinely universal problem.

But that would be far from the truth. The rise in petroleum prices was more a solution than a problem to the oil-producing states, like Saudi Arabia and Nigeria, that had banded together to create the OPEC cartel and to raise the prices in the first place. A number of those countries were literally awash in money, revenues they could scarcely absorb. This was also an immediate bonanza to the Western oil companies, their stockholders, managers, and employees, who for a time enjoyed record profits. The most dramatic contrast was between these economic winners and the most pathetic losers, the non-oil producing Third World countries that were heavily dependent on petroleum for fertilizers and for infant industries. The balance-of-payments deficits of some of these countries shot through the ceiling. The sudden rise in oil prices created economic shocks of great magnitude all over the world, but those shocks were experienced in radically different ways. One could not really say that this was experienced worldwide as a *common* problem. Indeed, creative efforts to deal with the problem were what finally began to create a problem among the oil producers, for diminishing demand for oil threatened the disruption of the cartel at last. Countries like Nigeria and Venezuela which had become dependent on the new flow of money found themselves unable to complete projects and service loans to which they had become committed.

The second economic problem for illustration is that posed by inflation and unemployment. Can we at least all agree that inflation and unemployment are common problems that we all have an interest in solving? That may be true when inflation and unemployment are so severe as to destroy an economy altogether. But short of that, there are clear beneficiaries of both inflation and unemployment. As a general rule, debtors tend to benefit from inflation as long as their income is basically keeping pace with it. Why? Because the currency they must repay is becoming steadily cheaper. But those who have made the loans will now receive less money back than they lent out, in real terms. The point can be illustrated poignantly in relation to the housing market in Western countries. Someone who had the good fortune to buy a house ten years ago with an 80 percent loan in many European or North American cities will have seen the value of that home double or treble in current terms, so that now the lender's share of the equity value of the home is only 25 or 30 percent where it would have been 50 or 60 percent without inflation. This bonanza for the homeowner, this "solution" to his or her economic problems, is a real "problem" not only for lending institutions that may be committed to low rates of interest negotiated years ago but also for young families who cannot even consider the purchase of a new home at today's inflated prices. Inflation redistributes wealth to a new set of "winners" and "losers." It might be hard to persuade the "winners" that this is a *problem!*

What about unemployment? In real terms, it is hard to see how any of us benefit when potentially productive human labor resources are idled. And yet, it is widely believed by economists and business leaders that some unemployment may be necessary to keep pressure for wage increases from developing ruinous and inflationary momentum. The standard "hard medicine" used to suppress inflation is to lower demand through government monetary and fiscal policies, thus increasing unemployment, and thus dampening the upward pressure of wages and prices. This is precisely what the Reagan and Thatcher governments of the United States and the United Kingdom did in the early 1980s.[10] In both countries the immediate effect of the "hard medicine" policies was a dramatic decrease in inflation. It was also a dramatic increase in unemployment. One does not have to be a genius to see here that solutions to problems for one set of people (possibly even the majority) are creating a whole new set of problems for another set of people (doubtless a minority, but a rather large one).

We could suggest still further illustrations, but the general point has been made. Economic life is not reducible to a series of problems that are experienced in common by all of us and that can be solved if we only bend our common will and creative intelligence to the task.[11] We cannot afford to neglect the value questions in the name of pure pragmatism. A great deal depends on how we define our problems in value terms, not just factual or technical terms. Much is at stake in our judgments about what is to be done, economically, and who is to get what. Above all, we cannot finally evade the question of priorities.

Conflicting Priorities

Drawing this together, it is clear that economic choices are not usually between the stark alternatives of good and evil. More often they force us to decide among possibilities, each of which is relatively good. Reinhold Niebuhr is supposed to have said that the really important questions in ethics are the ones involving relative judgments. If so, economic life is the quintessential arena for significant ethical decision-making. For here we are constantly dealing with questions of "more or less for this or that" and "who gets what?"

Later we will have to consider the views of those who believe that priorities are best established by allowing the free-market economy to operate on its own. That judgment itself involves some decisions about priorities, as we shall see. But whether one favors a highly independent free-market mechanism or outright governmental control over a planned economy (or something in between), the priorities questions must still be faced. Economics cannot do everything. It cannot satisfy every desire; it is debatable whether it can meet every need. We have to choose—either privately or socially, either actively or passively—which of the conflicting demands are most important. Some choices may seem obvious, others less so, although in our time the setting of priorities presents unusual complexities along with profound conflicts.

Some years ago a number of prominent writers addressed the theme of "goals of economic life" in a volume sponsored by the National Council of the Churches of Christ in the U.S.A.[12] The book is now dated by thirty years, and even at the time its conclusions were regarded as controversial. But the title suggests a timelessly important task for people who wish to address economic issues seriously: It is first important to get straight about what economic activity is supposed to accomplish, the "goals" it is supposed to serve. And then we can confront the problem of how to achieve those goals economically with greater effectiveness.

Economic priorities are social. This is not to say that the enhancement of individual freedom and creativity and the meeting of personal needs and desires have no place in the setting of economic priorities. It is to argue both that human beings are inescapably social in their very nature and that society inevitably is involved in the setting of priorities. It can be argued that economic life should be organized in such a way that individual freedom and creativity are truly supported. But it will be a social decision to arrange economic institutions in such a way that these individual values are accorded high priority.

In the next chapter we shall examine the question of who should be able

to set the priorities, before returning in subsequent chapters to the ethical/
theological frame of reference in which Christians and others of similar
moral persuasion should address the priority questions and to the substan-
tive issues themselves.

Points:
1) Economic priorities must be set according to social values
2) Values + priorities often conflict — often no community of interests
3) Perception of problems are relative to people w/ different views
4) Ethics deals w/ the good

1) What are priorities?
2) Who should set them? — this is prior question

CHAPTER TWO

Who Should Set Social Priorities?

Adam Smith's flash of genius was his recognition that the prices that emerged from voluntary transactions between buyers and sellers—for short, in a free market—could coordinate the activity of millions of people, each seeking his own interest, in such a way as to make everyone better off. It was a startling idea then, and it remains one today, that economic order can emerge as the unintended consequence of the actions of many people, each seeking his own interest.

—Milton and Rose Friedman, 1979[1]

The party directing and maintaining the favour of the masses does not need to be formed by all the people of the country. . . . They receive from the party the direction in which the people have to move.

—Canaan Sodido Banana, 1982[2]

A responsible society is one where freedom is the freedom of men who acknowledge responsibility to justice and public order, and where those who hold political authority or economic power are responsible for its exercise to God and the people whose welfare is affected by it.

—World Council of Churches, 1948[3]

Prior even to the question of what our priorities should be is the question of who should set them. As these few quotations suggest, even that is a hotly debated subject. Power questions always are vigorously debated, and the power to determine the goals and direction of economic life is unimaginably important. This question is center stage in the economic debates of the 1980s, and it will continue to be fought over for years to come. There are three broadly divergent kinds of answers to the question of who should decide on the priorities. Opting for one or another of these answers will not in itself tell us what the priorities ought to be, but it is a very important first step.

Letting the Free Market Decide

One option is suggested by the Milton Friedman quotation at the head of this chapter: "economic order can emerge as the unintended consequence of the actions of many people, each seeking his own interest." That statement echoes the famous view of Adam Smith:

> Every individual is continually exerting himself to find the most advantageous employment for whatever capital he can command. It is his own advantage, indeed, and not that of society, which he has in view. But the study of his own advantage naturally, or rather necessarily, leads him to prefer that employment which is most advantageous to the society. . . . he is led by an invisible hand to promote an end which was no part of his intention.[4]

This is a striking idea: *Nobody* should attempt to set priorities for the whole society. If each of us will just look after her or himself, that will also yield the best results for society as a whole. Smith argued that the free-market mechanism does what no individual or group of individuals could hope to do. It motivates everybody to contribute their best efforts, because otherwise they will not have anything to exchange. But it also leaves everybody free to exchange what they have for whatever they want, thereby assuring that the greatest good will result—by an "invisible hand." So priorities of production and distribution are both taken care of even though all participants in the economy are acting on the basis of their own interests as they understand them. In effect, nobody really has to care about what the economy is doing as a whole; that takes care of itself. And in a free-enterprise economy that is functioning properly it takes care of itself very well indeed.

The idea of laissez-faire (literally, leaving the economy alone to do its work through the free market) has exerted great influence in the Western world since *Wealth of Nations* was published in 1776. In its pure form it fell into disfavor during the decades of the 1930s through the 1960s, but it has enjoyed a remarkable resurgence in some countries in the 1970s and 1980s. In particular, the governments of Margaret Thatcher in the United Kingdom and Ronald Reagan in the United States have marked an abrupt return to laissez-faire policies. In one celebrated speech early in his administration, President Reagan reacted strongly against the use of government economic mechanisms to promote social objectives:

> The taxing power of government must be used to provide revenues for legitimate Government purposes. It must not be used to regulate the economy or

bring about social change. We've tried that and surely must be able to see it doesn't work.

Social change should be left to occur naturally. Free institutions, in particular the free market, will result in the most beneficial forms of social outcome. The Reagan and Thatcher governments found important intellectual support from the works of economists or social writers like Milton Friedman, George Gilder, and Michael Novak, all of whom support a high degree of economic freedom and all of whom believe that the best results occur in such an environment.[5] There are important differences among these writers, of course. But one is impressed by the impatience each of them expresses toward the social experiments of government over the past half-century. Do not look toward government for solutions to our problems, a Friedman will exclaim. Government itself *is* the problem![6] Each of these writers also argues that the central problem of economics is not the allocation of goods and services so much as it is the *creation* of goods and services. A Novak will remark that poverty requires no explanation; that is the natural state of humankind. It is wealth that should not be taken for granted and needs to be understood. We now know that the source of wealth is the creative, productive actions of free men and women acting under the challenges and disciplines of the free-enterprise system.[7] The liberation of the creative, productive energies of the human race should be the one economic priority. All else will flow from this. The role of competition is implicit in all this, but the neoconservative writers do not think of competition in negative terms. They see it as the only way to promote efficiency. In a free competitive market, would-be producers and sellers are vying with one another to provide the best goods and services at the lowest prices. The winners in that competition can only be winners by serving the interests of the buyers, which means the public in general. It is even disputed by some, such as George Gilder, whether governmental intervention is much needed to maintain competition. In the long run, Gilder argues, even monopolies bring forth competitive alternatives.[8]

How are we to assess these neoconservative claims? Is this really the best way to go about establishing social priorities, letting the market mechanism do it for us?

The neoconservatives make claims of a more or less pragmatic sort. They are convinced that this is the best way to motivate people to do what must be done to make an economy work. Even if one were to conclude that greedy sinfulness is at work in economic life, this system seems to offer the best prospect of enlisting that selfishness for constructive social ends. Only by serving others can one hope to make a profit in the free-enterprise system; that is, only by providing *other* people with what *they* want. Gilder even finds this exchange relationship to be an expression of love, not of self-centered greed.[9] But either way, the result is held to be constructive.

What about the concentrations of wealth that may then develop? There is some argument about the extent to which that really does occur, although there is no question that every capitalist society (and most socialist societies too) exhibits great inequalities. Does that mean that some people then are in a better position to determine the social priorities of all the rest? Most capitalist thinkers believe this to be greatly exaggerated. But sometimes this is portrayed as a strength, not a weakness. As long ago as Andrew Carnegie, the point was being advanced (particularly by him) that those who succeed in amassing wealth are also, by and large, the ones who can best be trusted to spend it wisely. They have already demonstrated both their creativity and their self-discipline. Insofar as they have disproportionate power in the determination of social objectives (such as the decisions about libraries and museums and universities—and even politics) there are some who would argue that that really is not so bad. Their decisions are most likely to exhibit vision and to be less tied to baser tastes and immediate consumption. But, the neoconservatives point to the most practical result of all. It is the free market that has proved to be the great engine of production, liberating humanity from the scourge of poverty.

Neoconservative writings, while asserting the sheer practicality of the free-market mechanism, also emphasize certain moral underpinnings. Above all, they celebrate personal freedom and the virtues of individualism. The respect for freedom has deep philosophical roots, most notably in Immanuel Kant's principle that every person should be treated as an end in him or herself, and not merely as a means. Where people are not accorded freedom to make their own choices and to live with the consequences of those choices they are generally made into the instruments of somebody else's choosing. They are reduced to subhuman status. Real love for people means holding their personhood in high esteem and protecting their freedom. Neoconservatives make much of the moral fallacy of paternalism. We may think we are doing people a favor by solving all their problems for them; actually, we are treating them as less than human and undermining their own self-respect and creative potential. Some people may misuse their freedom. If they do, they must not be spared the consequences, for that, too, undermines their moral dignity. So the ethical underpinnings of the neoconservative movement are not necessarily moral greed and selfishness. Gilder insists that it is love, not selfishness, at the foundation of the free-market system. You have to reach out toward others to make this system work, and the system itself is based on freedom and respect for persons.[10]

It is also based on a particular moral conception of property. Every society has some system of property rights, some way of determining use values when disputes arise, usually with some mixture between personal and family property and property held in common by and for the entire community. The free-market system, of course, emphasizes private property. The historical origins of this are doubtless complex. But John Locke's contribution to the shaping of the laissez-faire tradition of property rights is especially important. According to Locke,[11] property does not exist in the original "state of nature." Everything is from God and is equally available to everybody. But property is created when people withdraw things from the state of nature through their own labor. Wilderness belongs to no one in particular. But if I clear the land of trees, and plow and plant and cultivate it, I have created a farm. By "mixing" my labor with the resources of nature, I will have created property. My property. If I build a boat, using the raw materials of wood and metal and canvas, it is *my* boat. If I use the boat to catch fish, they are *my* fish. If I invent something or write something, it is *mine*. From this is derived my right to sell or trade what I have brought into being through my labor, and then, in turn, to own what I have received in exchange. Nobody has a right to take this property from me or to interfere with my right freely to buy and sell in the marketplace. Thus the basic Lockean conception as it has developed in capitalist culture.

In Locke's view, echoed in many ways by subsequent writers over the past three centuries, this conception of property is self-evident. After all, to whom *should* an object belong if not to the one who used her or his own labor to make it? It would not even exist, as a desirable thing, if somebody had not done this work. Nobody else has any claim on it. Taking this property away from its rightful owner is tantamount to stealing, in this view. And government itself, through burgeoning welfare programs, has become the foremost thief! Such programs take property away from some, who have earned it through their labor, to give it to others who have not done anything to deserve it. Neoconservatives regard this as immoral.

Thus, respect for persons and respect for property rights combine to form an ethical foundation for the view that people should be left alone to plan their own lives and their own priorities for themselves. Some will choose one thing, some another. Some will wish to work hard in order to accumulate enough goods for a comfortable life style or enough resources for travel, education, or other forms of personal enrichment. Others will place a higher premium on leisure, content to live simply but not to have to labor strenuously. Nobody should intervene to force people to adopt and work for priorities they do not care about.

Limitations to the Free-Market Mechanism

The case for allowing the free market to establish priorities is obviously persuasive to many people and, as we have said, it has enjoyed a resurgence in the past few years. Many more people, including even some socialists, believe that some use should be made of free-market institutions in the allocation of goods and services. But that would be as a part of a wider overall plan. Those who believe in real free-market allocation do not see this as part of a broader scheme; they see it as the place where the decisive priority-setting occurs. If they are right, then there is little point in further examination of values and social priorities—except, perhaps, in advising one another about the best stewardship of our own personal resources. There would be no vantage point from which one could see the whole picture and no leverage point at which policy decisions could be reached to implement economic priorities for the entire community. So we are facing a watershed issue when we decide for or against reliance on the market mechanism to establish our priorities for us.

During the first half of the twentieth century, most of the Western capitalist countries decided they simply could not rely on this mechanism, at least not without combining it with a good deal of social planning. Practically speaking, too many people were being hurt economically in the process and too many public concerns were being neglected. In retrospect, one wonders how on earth President Reagan could ever have concluded that it hasn't "worked" to use the taxing power of government for purposes of social change. If anything hasn't *worked*, it would appear to be overreliance on the free market to do everything.

Economic historian Karl Polanyi makes this point in considerable depth in his *The Great Transformation*.[12] The free-market mechanism did prove to be an enormous stimulus to production. It was indispensable to the breakup of medieval feudalism and to the emergence of the whole Industrial Revolution which, in turn, has been the source of vast increases in wealth and well-being. But the human consequences were often appalling. Polanyi finds it striking that despite broad intellectual agreement in the early nineteenth century on the virtues of laissez-faire capitalism, one after another of the societies committed to free-market principles found it absolutely necessary to intervene for the sake of people and social objectives that were not being served by those principles. In the case of England there was the somewhat ill-designed Speenhamland experiment involving income guarantees for unemployed and poorly paid people, with payments indexed to the price of bread.[13] Speenhamland was inefficient economically, a bit of a setback in the overall development of industrialism in England. But *in social terms* it was very important to protect vital social interests during the transition period. Otherwise, for all its efficiency, laissez-faire capitalism would have ripped the social fabric apart. Polanyi concludes from this and other evidence that "the concept of a self-regulating market was utopian, and its progress was stopped by the realistic self-protection of society."[14] He continues: "if market economy was a threat to the human and natural components of the social fabric, as we insisted, what else would one expect than an urge on the part of a great variety of people to press for some sort of protection? This was what we found."[15]

The outpouring of legislation in the Progressive and New Deal eras of twentieth-century America came in direct response to human need and social pressure. The exploitation of child labor (and of the labor of men and women), hazardous working conditions, dehumanizingly long hours of work, low wages, periodic times of depression with high unemployment, shoddy and dangerous products, ruin of the natural environment, racial, religious, and gender discrimination all evoked social exposé, popular outcry, and governmental intervention. Left alone, the free-market mechanism was increasing production all right, but it was devastating human society. It was widely perceived that some outside force had to intervene in the market to establish and protect social goals transcending sheer economic efficiency. It was as though society instinctively rebelled against the triumph of instrumental economic values over intrinsic social ones.

But the inadequacies of laissez-faire capitalism also extend to its ethical justification. The personalistic values of freedom and individual creativity are important ones, to be sure. But in their one-sided presentation is concealed a faulty understanding of human nature. Each of us is a unique individual, a center of freedom and creativity. But we are also social by nature. The most serious philosophical failing of laissez-faire capitalism is its neglect of the social nature of human beings. Neoconservatives are more aware than their predecessors were of the social reality, but their conception of society is one of exchange: you do this for me, and I will do that for you. Even George Gilder's claim that capitalism had its origins in primitive acts of giving suggests a kind of self-interested individualism: A few venturesome people give gifts to others in the hope (though not with the assurance) that they will return the favor.

> Through the gifts or investments of primitive capitalism, man created and extended obligations. These obligations led to reciprocal gifts and further obligations in a growing fabric of economic creation and exchange, with each

giver hoping for greater returns but not assured of them, and with each recipient pushed to produce a further favor. This spreading out of debts could be termed expanding the money supply.[16]

Similarly, the various writings of Ayn Rand portray society as the sum of the (largely economic) transactions of free and independent persons—although Rand is explicitly contemptuous of any display of altruism, whether or not it conceals an expectation of return.[17]

But human beings are not just individuals, and society is not just the sum of the individual transactions of people who have something to gain from one another. Human life is *shared* life. It is a sharing of perceptions and values and language and purposes and identity. We are born and nurtured in a social environment or we do not survive. Our very consciousness is mediated through language and the perception of others, to which we in turn contribute.

The neoconservatives have hold of half the truth, for no conception of human nature is adequate that neglects individual personhood, and no ethical vision is whole that neglects freedom. But the neglect of our social nature is a fatal error. Turned into an economic or political philosophy, it invites a kind of principled selfishness wherein people are led to believe that social good is only a byproduct of individual good and that it is a sufficient goal for each person to look out for him or herself.

Locke's view of property is also riddled with illusion, especially when attempts are made to apply it in the modern world. For one thing, we know in ways that Locke could scarcely have imagined that the natural world is limited. In his time the whole new continent of North America had opened up, with vast reaches of uncharted wilderness occupied and defended by a very small number of aboriginal inhabitants. It was easy enough for Locke to model a conception of property on the opportunity for settlers to stake out their claims in North America, to clear the land, and to till the soil. They only had to have the will to work. But that frontier is gone now, almost everywhere on earth. Now it is a question of access to the raw materials of nature, and not a question of imaginative labor alone.

But for another thing, Locke's individualism obscures the extent to which property is created socially. It is truly a difficult thing to sort out the relative importance of the contributions many people have made even to the solitary flash of an individual's genius, not to mention the obviously social character of mass production. It is asserted that the market will set wages and salaries in accordance with the actual contributions of each person to the process, but that is largely an illusion too. There is more evidence that wages are based upon a complex and largely inherited set of relationships and expectations derived only *somewhat* from the identifiable talents and contributions of individual workers or managers.[18]

Free-Market Efficiency as Social Inefficiency

There are other problems with relying on the free market alone to establish social priorities. These have to do with the market when it is most successful—when it is doing exactly what the theory says it is supposed to do.

First, there is the problem of how one is to achieve a much-desired social result from one's purely private transactions. Being geared to private exchange, the market creates a strong bias toward individual forms of consumption. But nobody wants to limit consumption to individual goods and services. The market performs best in providing food, clothing, shelter, entertainment, and other things we want and need. It is an awkward mechanism for providing communitywide facilities in education and recreation and communication. It is a virtually impossible mechanism for providing highways and national defense. It is possible to stretch the free-market model theoretically to cover all these things, with associations of private persons banded together to purchase land for highways, with all parks and recreation facilities handled like Disneyland, with all schools handled on a private basis along with fire and police protection, with due care being taken to ensure that everybody paid for exactly the goods and services received, and so on. Milton Friedman constructs such a utopian capitalist world in his *Capitalism and Freedom,* exempting only the most inextricably social needs and facilities from private ownership and market transactions and providing elaborate schemes of educational vouchers, etc., to keep everything competitive.[19] But why go at things in such an awkward way? It reminds one of the quip that some people know the cost of everything and the value of nothing. If the community is to realize itself as a community it has a stake in directing the economic process toward some kinds of ends, including those things the existence of which ought to be *guaranteed.* We all benefit from the overall quality of community life. It is quite impossible to calculate exactly the proportions by which each of us benefits over the course of time. And it seems ridiculous even to try to calculate such things. Relative priorities must be established and, doubtless also, some means of calculating the cost of social facilities and services relative to each other and to private forms of consumption. But the effort to calculate exactly what each social service is worth to each recipient or user seems fatuous on the face of it. More than that, it reveals a one-sidedly individualistic view of our humanity.

But there is another problem, present precisely when the market is functioning exactly as it is supposed to do—that is, when it is that form of disciplined efficiency the theory has always proclaimed it to be. Efficiency, in the pure model, is a result of the discipline of competition. Less efficient enterprises lose ground in their competition with more efficient ones. There is the strongest possible incentive to provide the market exactly what it wants (or can be induced to want) at the lowest possible price. Firms with high costs either destroy their own profit margins or no longer remain competitive. This often works out beneficially, in practice as well as in theory. Consumers find prices going down in competitive markets and quality going up. Entrepreneurs are motivated to develop new products to enrich the lives of people further.

But free-market competition also creates incentives to cut costs in ways that are damaging to people and to the community. The cheapest way to dispose of waste products is generally to dump them into the nearest stream or landfill or to let them belch forth into the skies without using expensive filtering devices or transporting them to safer places or refraining altogether from using productive techniques that threaten the environment. It also costs more to install safety devices on machinery and to pay more wages than the market strictly requires and to provide socially desirable fringe benefits. Irresponsible firms that evade such necessary costs may, thereby, secure favorable competitive markets. The market thus provides an incentive to irresponsible behavior when it saves money to be irresponsible. Somehow the rules of the game have to be structured in such a way that all participants are rewarded for good, not irresponsible, behavior. But that requires priority-setting from some vantage point outside the market mechanism itself. Somebody (or some group) has to decide whether the productive efficiencies gained by harmful practices are worth the costs to the community and to the people who face the impact of those practices most directly.

This point is routinely acknowledged in the literature of economics, which speaks of the costs that are borne by the public as "externalities." One standard text remarks that

> *Wherever there are externalities, a strong case can be made for supplanting complete individualism by some kind of group action:* consumers should be made to pay for the smoke damage that their purchases make inevitable, as would be the case if we supplanted laissez faire by a tax or by coercive ordinances; a conservation subsidy to farmers, that they will keep trees growing and thereby prevent disastrous floods hundreds of miles downstream, might represent rational social policy; regulations that prevent small-holders from digging oil wells frenziedly at the edge of their neighbors' property would be economically efficient. The reader can think of countless other

externalities where sound economics would suggest some limitations on individual freedom in the interest of all.[20]

Even more conservative economists, like Milton Friedman, quite agree
with the general point.[21] But sometimes they do not see its far-reaching
implications when it is understood that there are widespread social effects—good and bad—of economic activity and that the market mechanism itself does not begin to register them. What is "efficient" in market
terms may very well be profoundly inefficient in its effects on the wider
community. The market is therefore not a very good approach to establishing the community's scale of priorities, although it may be one helpful
part of that broader process.

Priority-Setting by Elites

If the free market is not an adequate way to go about setting social
priorities, what is? One obvious way to deal with that problem is to turn it
over to the people who really seem *qualified* to do it. We have already
noted that some capitalist thinking rather rejoices in the prospect that there
should be a high correlation between wealth and the power to make social
decisions. Andrew Carnegie put the matter clearly enough; some might
say even a bit crassly:

wealth, passing through the hands of the few, can be made a much more
potent force for the elevation of our race than if it had been distributed in
small sums to the people themselves. Even the poor can be made to see this,
and to agree that great sums gathered by some of their fellow-citizens and
spent for public purposes, from which the masses reap the principal benefit,
are more valuable to them than if scattered among them through the course of
many years in trifling amounts. . . . This, then, is held to be the duty of the
man of Wealth: . . . to consider all surplus revenues which come to him
strictly as trust funds, which he is called upon to administer in the manner
which, in his judgment, is best calculated to produce the most beneficial
results for the community—the man of wealth thus becoming the mere agent
and trustee for his poorer brethren, bringing to their service his superior
wisdom, experience, and ability to administer, doing for them better than
they would or could do for themselves.[22]

So candid an expression of aristocratic paternalism would not be considered in good taste today, but Carnegie's philosophy is at least latent when
it is held that public causes (libraries, symphony orchestras, museums,
universities) should generally be privately funded. Those who have the
resources are likely to be the ones best fitted to determine how the resources should be used. It may be that Carnegie, through his acknowledged benefactions, was more faithful in the actual execution of this philosophy than most rich people have been. His gifts to the public of

libraries, museums, institutions for learning and the promotion of peace, etc., did manifest a generous and visionary character. But Carnegie appears to be as much the exception as the rule. If the uses of money by the wealthy elite are not purely selfish they are as likely to be quixotic (what would one say about a Howard Hughes or even a J. Paul Getty, to name two extraordinarily wealthy men?). In truth, the skills and habits of mind entailed in amassing a fortune may not at all lend themselves to the broader service of human good; and some of the people with the wisest public vision have devoted themselves to public service and not to making money.

There are, of course, public or governmental elites as well. Social planning conjures up images of a Robert Moses literally transforming the face of New York City with his vast public works projects. It is popular sport to ridicule planners and bureaucrats and social engineers, and sometimes with good reason. One generation of elite planners may create the next generation's disaster. In the United States, urban high-rise public housing projects often seem to qualify for such criticism, as do some ventures in educational planning. In Britain, debate centers on economic planning. One senses that the resentment is as often directed at the paternalism or even arrogance with which some elites go about planning the lives and circumstances of all their fellow citizens as it is disapproval of the choice of priorities. But it is also the case that elitism in social planning always looks better if one is in the elite or if one can designate the elite than if one is on the outside looking in. There are usually several competing versions of utopia at any one time, each claiming the authority of genuine rationality. It would all be easier if there were a generally acknowledged class of experts upon whom all could agree and (most important of all) experts who could be counted on to agree among themselves.

Marxism maintains that there is a scientific analysis of society which provides humanity with the truly authentic picture of the direction of history. The historic role of the Communist Party is to give leadership in facilitating that all-important revolutionary transformation of society. The party does not include all members of society; it is in fact always a rather small percentage of the population in Marxist societies. But the party— actually the leadership of the party—considers itself to be the representative of the true interest of all the masses. This version of scientific socialism is familiar to all students of European Communist parties. Third World Marxist liberation movements generally have a more populist character, with some effort to consult the peasantry in the decision-making and priority-setting process. But even here there is often more than a touch of elitism. Note again the statement by Canaan Sodido Banana, the president of Zimbabwe, at the head of this chapter: "The party directing and maintaining the favour of the masses does not need to be formed by all the people of the country." To qualify for party membership, one must have qualities of leadership and "other attributes not readily available to all." In his personal life President Banana has provided striking support for egalitarianism (even turning part of the beautiful grounds of his presidential palace into an agricultural and poultry cooperative, with himself working alongside others as an ordinary member). But he also clearly believes that true knowledge of the appropriate direction for society is only available for some people, and they should provide the leadership for all the rest.

If everybody agreed with the Marxist vision (if even all the Marxists agreed among themselves), it would make it easier for us to say that the party elite should set the priorities for all of us. But there is no such consensus, and the countries under Marxist domination have been all too ready to run roughshod over dissenters. Equality of opportunity to participate in the political process and freedom of expression are values that do not have high priority in most of these settings. Some people are believed to know best, and they are willing enough to insist that everybody else conform.

Laissez-faire critics of all forms of social planning have a strong point when they criticize elitism as showing disrespect for human beings. To a lesser degree they also have something of a point in noting the inefficiencies that often accompany both left- and right-wing paternalism. They are usually blind to the same elitist paternalism when it develops in a free-market setting, and they are complacent about the negative results of reliance upon that setting to establish social priorities automatically. Is there no other way?

Social Priorities in the Responsible State

The socialist Michael Harrington once observed that if the state owns the economy it is a very important question "who owns the state."[23] If, somehow, social priorities have to be established by and for the whole society, it is critically important how the people who are affected by this are to be involved in the process. Will they ultimately "own" it? Will decisions be made in their name without their being consulted?

Any conceivable approach to the setting of social priorities, from the free market of laissez-faire capitalism to the highly planned and centralized socialist state, is bound to have outcomes that are offensive to many people. Society is closely enough integrated that we are all affected by the decisions of others.

But it does make a difference whether everybody has the opportunity to participate in the process of decision-making. The laissez-faire school asserts that everybody does have that right in the free-market system, voting, as it were, with their decisions as workers and consumers. But the number of such "votes" available to different people is grossly inequitable. We vote with our dollars (or pounds, or yen, or lire), but some people have many more dollars than others and some have scarcely any at all. Decisions reached by the marketplace do not reflect the democratic outcome implied by those who speak of the democracy of the marketplace.

Moreover, as we have seen, it is awkward to the point of impossibility for people to use their consumer and labor "votes" to set priorities for public consumption, even if that is what they most want to do. People cannot take their individual resources and go out and buy a rapid transit system for their city—nor can most afford to buy parks or streets or police and fire protection. Theoretically they can respond, with their money, to the imaginative entrepreneur who establishes widely desired institutions or services. But the result is awkward, piecemeal, and sometimes profoundly destructive when taken as the sole approach to the provision of social institutions and services. There needs to be an arena of decision-making in which all can participate in making those crucial decisions of social priority which affect the quality of life available for each and all.

This is exactly what the First Assembly of the World Council of Churches meant when, through its call for a "Responsible Society," it defined such a society in part as one where "those who hold political authority or economic power are responsible for its exercise to God and the people whose welfare is affected by it."[24] Most of the neoconservatives doubt that this can be done. They are inclined to regard government as being inescapably irresponsible, at least when it deals with economic questions. A governmental bureaucracy, like the Marxist party, may claim to speak for all the people, but conservative critics believe that in actual fact the bureaucracy is beyond social control. It can do what it wishes with the people's tax money—even using that money to perpetuate itself in power against their wishes. It, the bureaucracy, represents a large and powerful interest group, a "new class" with identifiable interests and with all the necessary means at hand to preserve and enhance them. Unlike business corporations it does not have to confront the disciplines of the market, and unlike the politicians it does not even have to run for reelection.

There is some truth in every caricature, including this one. But that is still a largely inaccurate caricature of what actually happens in the governments of democracies like the U.S. and Canada and Britain. All such countries have large numbers of dedicated public servants who are ultimately accountable to elected officials and, through them, to the people at large. In nearly twenty years of living and working at the seat of the U.S. government in Washington, D.C., I have observed several things about how the federal bureaucracy relates to the elected government and to the people:

1. The harshest criticisms of the civil service sometimes occur not because the "bureaucracy" is unconcerned about the public interest, but because it *is* concerned. Regulatory agencies may be fully responsive to the real political will of the vast majority of the people—for instance, in enforcing regulations to protect the environment or to preserve occupational safety—but that will not spare them criticism from those whose freedom to pollute or to endanger has been constricted.

2. When government agencies appear to be defending selfish interests (which, often enough, they do), they may in fact be reflecting, not resisting, the wider political process. It is interesting to observe how this or that governmental agency can be related to particular political leaders and, through them, to particular popular constituencies. Often the most powerful leaders of legislative committees have determinative influence in the particular agencies related to the work of those committees. The chairperson of the Senate Agriculture, Nutrition, and Forestry Committee is likely to have substantial influence in the Department of Agriculture, the chairperson of the Armed Services Committee similarly in the Pentagon, and so on. Is this irresponsible? It may well be. But the power wielded by the legislator is part of an intricate balance of power as interest confronts interest on Capitol Hill. Agricultural policies favorable to the people of Iowa or North Dakota (as represented by lawmakers from those states) may be supported indirectly if not directly by legislators from New York and Pennsylvania in return for similar support for grants for major cities, and so on.

3. Civil servants lacking strong political support are usually forced to give way when their policies or procedures are challenged by Congress. They can sometimes be resourceful in protecting their budgets and even in squirreling away reserves for unclear purposes, provided nobody cares enough to scrutinize or challenge what is going on. But they can be and not infrequently are stopped cold by law and by the withholding of budgetary support—if there really is a political will to do so.

4. The civil service is a much-needed source of competence and continuity in informing and giving force to the public will. Without this instrument the public truly would be frustrated.

I suspect similar observations could be made in London, Ottawa, Bonn, or any other capital city of a Western democracy—along with some non-Western ones as well.

Bureaucracy, whether private or governmental, is an inescapable fact of life in the modern world. Much of the setting and implementing of social priorities will inevitably be done by bureaucracies. The real question is whether they are truly accountable to the public will. The shortcomings of the market as final arbiter of social priorities mean that we shall be driven, in the final analysis, to turn the direction of society over to some irresponsible, perhaps even faceless, elite unless we can find ways to adopt our most fundamental goals democratically. Even at best, the democratic process is undoubtedly more complicated than is suggested by idealized accounts of it. But when it is reasonably open and healthy, that process can do two things: It can establish and review the most important social priorities, and it can choose leaders who will reflect the values of those who elected them and be accountable to the people.

In respect to the first of these points, the electorate of most modern societies is too large and diverse to decide every question directly. For instance, in a typical congressional or parliamentary election only a handful of the literally thousands of potential issues are ever debated. But in a good election, it is the ''watershed'' issues that determine the outcome—the issues that represent fundamental choices between alternative values and directions and that represent a basic ordering of social priorities. These priorities do not have to extend to questions of detailed implementation; that can be left to the public servants and that will continue to be under review. Similarly, elected officials only represent a small proportion of the public service, but they are the ones who set the tone for the whole enterprise. The choice of who shall govern rarely comes down to a mechanical weighing of how candidates stand on all the issues. Stands on issues are important, but they point beyond themselves to deeper questions of character and values. Instinctively people ask whether particular candidates hold the same basic values and, if so, whether they will be effective in translating those values into the community's actual social priorities.

As all of this relates to economic issues, it should be evident that there could be either a democratic capitalism or a democratic socialism or some mixture of the two. But for either capitalism or socialism to warrant the label ''democratic,'' the economic order must finally be accountable to the political order, and the political order must be democratic. When Michael Novak writes of the "spirit of democratic capitalism" he does not seem quite clear about this point. While acknowledging that the "political system has many legitimate roles to play in economic life,"[25] Novak wishes to protect the autonomy of the economic from the political sphere in a pluralistic, not unitary, society. It is, no doubt, the better part of wisdom to protect areas of economic freedom. But the question which aspects of economic life should be relatively autonomous and which should not be is itself a political question before it is an economic one. One democratic society may come up with a different mix of public and private spheres of economic life from another, equally democratic society. But for the society to be democratic, that is a question that the community as a whole has to decide. There is no natural order of spheres to which we can refer for a determination of how economic life should be ordered.

We may note in passing that economic life in a number of democratic Western countries is more accountable to the people than it is in most of the officially Marxist societies. In the latter, the Communist Party claims to embody the true will and interest of "the masses," but there are no effective channels of political review and accountability whereby these "masses" are empowered to affect economic priorities fundamentally. These democratic Western countries are largely capitalist, but in principle these countries could at any time be transformed into socialist states by the adoption of appropriate laws. Short of that, these countries have political systems through which any economic question can be reviewed. The fact that these countries are in fact more accurately described as "mixed economies" (rather than pure capitalist ones) already helps make the point. For mixed economies are ones in which there exists a substantial public sector alongside the private market, with government acting as regulator, producer, and distributor of goods and services to a substantial extent. In all of these countries, the governmental involvements in economic life reflect the outcome of many political battles fought over a long period of history and with substantial public involvement.

What about those who disagree with the outcomes of the democratic process? Questions of social priority are rarely decided by unanimous consensus. There truly is a sense in which the social priorities of the majority are usually "forced" on those who oppose them. It should be news to no one that social life in general imposes the discipline of having to accept things that one would prefer not to accept, and that is preeminently true of the political order. The issue is not whether one is or is not "forced" to accept the priorities of others with which one is not in agreement. That will inevitably happen from time to time to everybody, regardless of the political and economic system. The important question is whether or not the outcomes are a fair representation of majority views and whether those who are in opposition are free to express their opposition through speech and press and organized political action. The question is whether today's defeated minority viewpoint can hope to persuade enough people to become tomorrow's majority opinion.

Good democratic theory is thus not limited to the proposition of majority rule; it also includes those minority rights without which an opposition could never express itself. We may be coerced into accepting certain priorities in the national budget that we find repugnant, but we may not be coerced out of the political process itself.

Are Democratic Decisions Necessarily Wise Ones?

The results of the democratic process can, of course, be deplorable. George Bernard Shaw once remarked, however, that while democracy may not be the best form of government, it is that form under which we best can guarantee that people will get what they deserve. Overall, the wisdom of democratic decision-making can be compared without embarrassment to that of any alternative form, but that does not mean that grievous errors and injustices will not ever occur. Even Shaw's remark misses the point that those who lose in the democratic process may not at all deserve the folly visited on the whole society by an unwise majority. But still, it is the process that best reflects the mind of the community, whereby the community's true priorities can best be given effect. And it is the process that is most open to the correction of its previous errors.

Favors democratic control of economic priorities for social ends.

CHAPTER THREE

A Theological Basis for Social Priorities[1]

Nine-tenths of what we see is behind our eyes.
—Old Chinese Proverb

It is an essential doctrine of Christianity that the world is fundamentally good and practically bad, for it was made by God, but is now controlled by sin. If a man wants to be a Christian, he must stand over against things as they are and condemn them in the name of that higher conception of life which Jesus revealed. If a man is satisfied with things as they are, he belongs to the other side.
—Walter Rauschenbusch (1907)[2]

Our perceptions of the world and of its problems are very largely formed by our values. The perspective we bring to bear very largely shapes what we see. I do not wish to argue that we are incapable of seeing and acting on reality as it really is, but our grasp of what reality *means* is always decisive. Certainly that is crucial for our assessment of problems and priorities. Where do our values come from? Answering that is an extraordinarily difficult thing. The whole social environment as we experience it from birth is laced with values, and those values have long and complex histories. Sometimes we are attracted to new values and change our lives to conform to them. Perhaps more frequently we inherit and acquire them unconsciously.

H. Richard Niebuhr observes perceptively that behind our specific and relative values, we have a "center of value" on the basis of which the lesser values gain their meaning.[3] That center of value is our "god," the object of our worship and loyalty. It may be the monotheistic faith of the Hebrew-Christian tradition, but it may also be our most fundamental group loyalty or the little idolatries of what Niebuhr calls polytheistic faith. The center of value is what ultimately gives meaning and shape to our lives. It is our theological frame of reference, for it is based on what we ultimately worship and believe. Our theological frame of reference is very important—even decisive—in determining what matters to us in all aspects of life, including economics. To accept this, we need not be believers in any one particular theological viewpoint. But everybody believes in something; everyone has some values that supersede and give point to other values; everyone has a center of value, a theological orientation. Sometimes that theological orientation is not the credal tradition to which one formally subscribes; sometimes it is. But whatever one's acknowledged religious views, the decisive question that serves to locate our *real* theology is, What do we value most?

Theological Entry Points

How are we to "apply" theology to economics and the determination of social priorities? Often enough Christians have thought they could find specific biblical texts to apply directly to specific contemporary problems. The Parable of the Talents (Matt. 25:14–30) could be taken as a mandate for capitalistic enterprise and St. Paul's "If any one will not work, let him not eat" (2 Thess. 3:10b) could be treated as a judgment against welfare programs. Such applications of these passages are questionable on exegetical grounds,[4] and an honest use of Scripture would also have to deal with the many biblical passages condemning wealth and the exploitation of the poor. Specific texts may be important parts of the tradition, but applying them directly to contemporary problems can greatly distort our perspective. Some of the particular passages now quoted to settle contemporary issues were never intended to have that kind of use, even at the time of writing. And those passages that did speak to such problems in their own time may be misleading when applied too directly to current issues today. It is debatable, for instance, whether St. Paul actually supported the institution of slavery (some passages suggest that he did, or at least that he did not challenge it in his advice to slaves). But whether he did or not, it would greatly distort our understanding of how Christianity should be related to economics if we were to use such passages to justify slavery in our own time. Biblical writings speak on different levels. Some convey the core meanings of the faith, while others apply those meanings to the ancient situation.

Those who wish to apply the faith tradition to contemporary issues as profoundly as possible will struggle first to understand the core meanings and then reflect creatively on how those meanings illuminate contemporary issues.

To do this, we need to seek the theological "entry points" that help relate the core meanings of faith to the most important underlying social and economic issues. These entry points are refractions from the central light; they are ways of seeing the core theological truth when we allow contemporary issues to pose important questions for theological response. Such an approach to theological application is largely intuitive and creative, but that does not mean that it is merely subjective. The faith tradition and the factual world are objective reference points. But the faith tradition is profound; it challenges ever-deepening levels of understanding and application. And since the factual world itself is almost infinitely complex, we should always be modest about the finality of our judgments.

Bearing this in mind, I wish to suggest six useful theological entry points into economic life and the setting of social priorities. These points are drawn generally from the biblical faith of a Christian, it being recognized that different Christians may wish to approach any or all of these points in different ways. The six points are not offered as a complete theology of society or economics, nor can we even explore these points completely. Nevertheless, such entry points can help us work toward a theological perspective on the issues of our time.

1. *Physical Existence as God's Creation.* Were theology to be committed to an altogether spiritual conception of life, it could dispense readily enough with economics. At best, the material world would be completely neutral or a kind of necessary evil. There would be no point in pursuing its meaning on a theological plane. But the mainstream of Christianity has persistently rejected an exclusively spiritualistic self-understanding, from the time of early Gnosticism to the present. Against spiritualism it has affirmed the doctrine of creation.[5] The material world is good because God created it to reflect good purposes. The theme is struck forcefully in the Genesis accounts of creation, in a number of the great nature psalms, in the Sermon on the Mount, and elsewhere in Scripture. While the goodness of the created material world is affected by recognition of evil, the doctrine of creation commits theology to a basically positive attitude toward economic life and material well-being. Material life is not evil; it is a good to be embraced, enhanced, and celebrated as God's gift.

2. *The Priority of Grace Over Works.* Biblical faith is covenantal through and through, which means that it understands human life to be in personal relationship with the source of all being. It is this personal relationship that confers ultimate meaning on both individual and social existence. We matter because we matter to God; and we are sisters and brothers in a moral community because we are the family of God. Our relationship with God and our relationships with one another are moral in quality.

They are in fact the essence of morality. Yet they are not moral because of our own moral initiative but rather because of God's gift. As expressed most profoundly in the parables of Jesus and the writings of St. Paul, God's love is the "given" with which we start. It is not something we have to earn in order to receive: "for he makes his sun rise on the evil and on the good, and sends rain on the just and on the unjust" (Matt. 5:45). St. Paul uses the juridical metaphor to say that we are saved by grace and not by works of the law. We are affirmed by God even before we have done anything to deserve it. Indeed, Paul argues that none of us *do* deserve what we receive. Those who take pride in their moral accomplishments tend to be self-righteous, and self-righteousness is in fact the most insidious spiritual danger of all. When we are self-righteous we are unable to respond gratefully to the goodness of life as a gift and we are estranged from our brothers and sisters whom we judge to be morally inferior to ourselves.

While the pertinence of this to economic life might not appear self-evident, the relationship of "grace" to "works" is an issue of watershed importance. If justice, ultimately, is only the proper rewarding of behavior, then we have a clear paradigm for economic organization. People should simply get what they "deserve," nothing more, nothing less. But on the other hand, if justice is patterned in accordance with the priority of grace, then economic goods should be produced and distributed in such a way as to enhance human well-being and self-acceptance and communal fellow feeling without asking first whether people have deserved what they receive. We shall want to take particular note of this when we discuss the poverty problem and what is to be done about it.

3. *Physical Well-Being and Social Relationship.* An important corollary of the foregoing points is that economics must be concerned about two things at once: the physical needs of people and the effect of economic organization on relationships. Both are important. Physical deprivation obviously frustrates human fulfillment. Without adequate food, clothing, shelter, and medical care people suffer and die, and one does not have to be an economist or a theologian to recognize that the purposes of human life are endangered. But economic life can also be structured in such a way that barriers are created between people, frustrating the higher ends of human community. Neither of these things—the physical and the relational—should be neglected. Each is, to some extent, independent of the other. The poorest members of a community may be well enough off economically that they are not suffering physically while, at the same time, they are so much poorer than others that it is nearly impossible to relate as brother and sister to the very affluent. On the other hand, it is at

least theoretically possible for everybody in the community to be deprived
to the point of physical suffering while the bonds of community itself
remain intact. So it is not even possible to establish a necessary ordering
of priorities between these two things, with physical well-being always
coming first. A case can be made that without physical well-being nothing
else is possible. But a case can also be made that the moral quality of life
in community is worth considerable sacrifice in physical well-being. Of
course, from a theological standpoint it is highly desirable to have both
physical well-being and good social relationships at the same time.

4. *Vocation.* The doctrine of vocation is a particularly good theological
entry point to the significance of work. The term means "calling," of
course; and the traditional implication of vocation was that it reflected
one's call from God. Post-Reformation Christianity generally understood
this to mean that everyone has a particular calling from God. Stated most
generally, the meaning is that we should be active in our grateful response
to God's gifts of life and love, and that our response should involve our
dedication to the realization of God's loving purposes. Hebrew faith and
Christian faith are, alike, activist. The theme of peaceful rest is also
biblical, but rest is always related to work in the portrayal of human
fulfillment. We rest in order to work as much as we work in order to rest.
It is the doctrine of vocation, indeed, that saves the Christian conception
of grace from leading to merely passive conceptions of existence. We are
not just passive receptacles of God's goodness; we are invited, through
grace, into creative activity. St. Paul is particularly careful not to push this
to the opposite extreme of seeing "salvation" as something we accomplish through our own efforts. We do not have to earn or deserve God's
grace in order to have it given to us; but God's grace remains unfulfilled
in our lives without active response on our part.

The connecting point between this and economic life is fairly obvious,
in light of the importance of work for the production and distribution of
goods and services. But the theological understanding of vocation is both
narrower and broader than a purely economic conception of work. It is
narrower in that some economic activities are so injurious to the life and
well-being of the community that they could never be regarded as vocational in the theological sense. Production and distribution of cocaine or
heroin is "economic" in that sense, but usually not vocational. But
vocation is also broader than a purely economic conception of work in that
some very useful activity falls outside normal definitions of gainful employment. Many people do good things without being paid to do them,
including voluntary service in community youth organizations or church
groups. It is a good thing when, within the normal working of the econ-

omy, all people are challenged to contribute their best creative efforts to the betterment of all.

5. *Stewardship.* The doctrine of stewardship has traditionally addressed the question of ownership and use of property. A more limited Protestant conception of stewardship has seen this as the giving of a certain portion of one's income, perhaps ten percent, to ecclesiastical institutions. But the doctrine of stewardship is more sweeping than that. It is recognition that everything belongs to God: "The earth is the Lord's and the fulness thereof, the world and those who dwell therein" (Psalm 24). All other property claims are relativized by that very basic one. An orderly society will, of course, define and protect the property rights of individuals and groups. But the theological perspective of stewardship does not permit us to treat those socially defined property rights as absolute or as derived from some natural order of things (as John Locke's view of property did). Property rights are morally, if not legally, subordinated to the purposes of the Creator. Property is to be enjoyed; but when it is understood in the light of stewardship, it is to be used for loving and not selfish purposes.

Furthermore, the perspective of stewardship respects the meaning of other sentient beings and of future generations. It does not consider the impertinent question, What has posterity ever done for me?[6] For stewardship recognizes the linkage of all generations through the common source of all being, and it accepts responsibility to the ultimate design of things and not only to oneself and a narrow range of loyalties.

6. *Original Sin.* There is, finally, the theological recognition that human nature is corrupted by self-centeredness. All people are presumed to be sinners. This does not mean that people are *exclusively* sinful, for they are also capable of generosity and love. But our tendency toward selfishness is painfully and persistently part of our makeup. The most persuasive theological accounts of original sin do not attribute this to our created nature or to moral weakness, as such, but rather to our despair and insecurity that lead us to frantic quests for self-fulfillment.[7] In our attempts to overcome our own deep feelings of insecurity we are almost driven to be utterly preoccupied with ourselves, to accumulate possessions, to dominate other people. For us to become loving, unselfish people requires a real "letting go" in faith. And that is difficult until we find ourselves grasped by a reality larger than ourselves. It is hard to love without being loved first.

The tendency toward self-centeredness has important implications for economics. It suggests that no economic system predicated entirely on human goodness is likely to be successful and that economics, as well as politics, needs to institutionalize protections against the destructive possibilities of self-centered behavior. It also suggests that we do well not to separate the world into "good" people and "bad" people. Original sin really means that *all* of us have this tendency and that no one can be presumed to have a corner on goodness. Self-righteousness, besides exhibiting the subtlest forms of sin, is often the root of the most demonic practices. Economically successful people need especially to be on guard lest they attribute their success to their own goodness while blaming poverty on the character deficiencies of poor people.

Theological Danger Signals

These brief theological characterizations suggest how a theological tradition can be explored in search of the most promising points of contact with economic issues. While they represent an interpretation of Christian faith, not all Christians are likely to accept each (or even any) of them. Still, this kind of exploration may encourage others to see how *their* theological perspectives afford entry points into economic life and the problem of priority-setting. Some, though not Christian, may find the foregoing points surprisingly close to their own perspectives and, if so, no Christian should be astonished to discover that his/her faith has elements that are regarded as universal even by others. For example, non-Christians can have a high conception of the goodness of the physical world and a deep sense of the universality and tragedy of human self-centeredness. They can even have some kind of conception of the importance of what Christians call "grace," and they can share the notion that the formative gifts of life are given before they are earned.

But without elaborating these points, the relevance of Christian theological entry points to economic life can be shown further by highlighting several points where contemporary economic attitudes can be challenged. I wish to suggest three such points in particular.

1. First, there is the persistent idolatry of materialism or of particular economic systems. The material realm becomes idolatrous when it is treated as an end and not as a means. Seen through theological eyes, there is a good deal of idolatry in all economic systems and in economic views expressed on all sides of the ideological spectrum. Inflated assessments of capitalism or socialism may contain much truth, but it is pathetic to treat them as absolute truth. Humanity is not on earth to serve economics; rather the function of economics is to serve humanity, in accordance with God's loving purposes. This is not to say that all economic systems are equally good, but that they should not be ultimate objects of loyalty. Recognition of this should give us reason to be somewhat more open in our attitudes toward the worldwide debate between contending economic ideologies.

2. The second point concerns property. A purely natural theory of property may have all the force of self-evident truth—as we have seen John Locke's theory to have—yet be in serious tension with the theological conception of stewardship. Whatever may be said for Locke's view, it is a self-centered one. In its individualism it neglects the grand design. Curiously, the underlying view of what constitutes property (the mixing of labor with things in the state of nature) also is suggested by Marxism, but there in a more social form. The Marxist criticism of alienation or exploitation very much depends on the view that what one has created through one's own labor has been taken away.[8] But whether in Marxist or Lockean form, the view that one's labor constitutes property treats nature itself simply as a given. But nature is not just a given. It is not unlimited. Those who control it have a much better opportunity to create property by mixing their labor with it. And in any event, a theological view of nature requires us to come to terms with the enduring source of nature's existence: "The earth is the Lord's."

3. A third theological problem is suggested by inflated theological images of the motivations presupposed by free-market activity or by socialism. Thus, George Gilder's attribution of capitalism ultimately to acts of outgoing, self-giving love[9] and Michael Novak's characterization of the corporation as sacramental in character and as fulfilling the biblical role of "suffering servant" in face of the ill-founded abuse of corporate critics.[10] How much truth is there, really, in such characterizations? Do businesspersons work fundamentally for the sake of others? Is there no hint of desire for reward clouding their motives? Are they willing to do all, to give all, without any specific material incentives? No doubt, there are numbers of business people whose motives include lovingkindness and concern for others. But are there not also those who are profoundly corrupted by materialism? And which of us, indeed, is altogether free of selfishness? Can business people claim to be?

Similarly, one can question the inflated conceptions of socialist morality that one sometimes hears—the new socialist man or woman of China or Cuba or wherever. For in such places, too, one can be infected by selfishness: in relation to the possession of power and prestige if not wealth. (For what it may be worth, my own journeys into socialist countries on three continents have not revealed any startling new developments in human nature, even though several of those countries have established impressive programs for human betterment.) It is a risky thing to assume that any people will, by virtue of their roles in systems and institutions, be wholly free of selfishness—whether those institutions are socialist or capitalist in character. A more modest expectation is that some institutions may help more than others in bringing out the best in people and in subordinating the destructive aspects of human sinfulness. A persuasive case can be mounted for both socialism and capitalism along these lines, but in neither instance would the case be dependent on fundamental changes in human nature itself.

In short, a theological perspective can help liberate one from the idolatries and illusions of the economic struggle. It can challenge us to keep our intrinsic and instrumental values in the right relationship so that the priorities we build into our personal economic lives and our social policies will undergird the deeper meaning of existence. That is not an easy proposition. We should not expect to develop a list of once-and-for-all priorities that will faithfully represent our theological orientation. The setting of priorities is a constant struggle to be faithful in which we learn from our failures as well as from our successes.

General Priorities

Before dealing with the practical questions of priority-setting that face us today, as we must do in later chapters, I wish to note two general priorities that are more or less implied by this theological discussion. These general priorities should be particularly helpful in shaping our more specific discussions later.

The *first general priority* is to make it possible for everyone to be able to function as a member of the community. It should be possible for all to have a sense of belonging, to be accepted by others, to participate responsibly in the community's life and decision-making.

Theologically, that priority is founded on the relationship we all have with the Creator and on the belief that we are all ultimately one family in God. That priority must take precedence over primarily individualistic or competitive conceptions that subordinate the reality of community. It is not as though one were choosing to subordinate the individual to the community, for the fulfillment of our being as individuals is through community, and respect for the dignity of persons as persons is an enduring criterion of healthy communal life. But giving priority to the community means that we can never reduce the meaning of our life together to a zero-sum game in which each is simply given the opportunity to carve out his or her well-being at the expense of others.

We cannot, of course, assume that people really will accept one another in the life of community. There is a spiritual reality involved here that cannot in any simple way be caused or created by social actions or policies. And yet the priority of making it possible for all to participate in the community can still serve as the direction for social policy. Some conditions aid while others impede the realization of this priority. That seems

obviously the case in respect to different kinds of law. Laws protecting
freedom of assembly and expression and freedom from arbitrary search
and arrest clearly help make it possible for authentic communal life to
develop. Oppressive laws, on the other hand, create barriers. When the
force of law maintains racial discrimination (as in the apartheid laws of
South Africa or the old "Jim Crow" laws in the United States), real
community is fragmented. But when laws protect equal access to public
facilities of all kinds, an important condition is present for the realization
of community. The presence or absence of such laws is not what actually
constitutes community life, for that involves human attitude and response
going beyond the legal structure. But one can speak meaningfully about
the presence or absence of legal conditions that are conducive to community.

That is also true of economic conditions. Later we will want to look
more closely at the significance of poverty, but here let it be noted that it is
possible to be so bereft of economic resources that one simply cannot be a
part of the community. And it is possible for there to be such enormous
gaps between wealth and poverty within a society that it is virtually impossible for human fellow feeling to bridge the chasm. Economics is
complex, and the relationship between economic processes and social
reality can be very subtle. We will not want to oversimplify those relationships as ideologues of right or left are prone to do. But we do need to be
very clear that whatever economic policies are most conducive to the
participation of everybody as an accepted, functioning member of the
community should have very high priority.

The *second general priority* is to arrive at the right balance between security and incentive. The first part of that is related to placing grace before
works, as discussed above. It is always a tempting thing for those who govern
to motivate people through their insecurities and vulnerabilities. It tends to
work. It produces the desired forms of behavior. People whose basic existence is made to depend on their performance are likely to perform, and those
who do not provide a good example to others through their suffering. But
behavior, as such, is not our ultimate objective. Community is more than
what people can be forced to do; it is what people *are,* to themselves and to
others. Motivation through deep-seated anxieties undermines the deeper
springs from which our true humanity flows. Positive motivations, rooted in
self-acceptance and loving relationships, lead to real fulfillment in community. Economic policy cannot be what a Christian means by "grace" in any
simple way. But by undergirding everybody's sense of security it can become
an important condition for grace.

I have spoken, however, about the right "balance" between security and incentive. Isn't security enough? It probably is not. In every known society there have had to be some incentives specifically designed to motivate good behavior and to discourage its opposite. The Christian anarchist tradition (as represented by Leo Tolstoy) and the contemporary libertarian movement are both wrong in supposing that the removal of restraints will automatically assure positive human response. Human nature is not simply good; there remains more truth than we might wish in the doctrine of original sin—and that also has implications for social policy. If there is a tendency toward self-centeredness in each of us, then social policy had better take that into account and correct for it. In part it does so by making the consequences of antisocial behavior undesirable (through use of *negative* incentives), and in part it does so by the use of rewards for socially desirable actions (*positive* incentives). In both cases, regrettably, rewards or punishments of an external sort are used to motivate behavior that might better be done for its own sake. Social service for the sake of the good it represents is better than social service for the sake of some other kind of reward. It is faint praise for any society that its people do good because they are afraid of punishment or because of the money or recognition they hope to receive. One is reminded of the searching question posed by one of T. S. Eliot's poems:

> When the Stranger says: "What is the
>   meaning of this city?
> Do you huddle close together because
>   you love each other?"
> What will you answer? "We all
>   dwell together
> To make money from each other"? or
>   "This is a community?"[11]

The latter answer is the preferable one, from the standpoint of Christian ethics, but the former accounts for much of the motivation in any modern city.

The remarkable psychological insight in Paul's contrast between grace and works is that people are only able to respond freely and creatively and lovingly if they can have faith that they have first been accepted and loved for what they are, not for what they have done. Only then can people respond, as it were, from the heart. A real "community," in the sense of Eliot's poem, is founded on mutual love, not on mutual self-interest.[12] So social policy needs partly to reflect the community's acceptance of all its people in a kind of secular expression of grace, and that is best done through the way it provides security in the conditions of life and livelihood.

But how can the provision of security and the need for some incentives be kept in creative tension? People who take both seriously will have to continue to wrestle with the problem. It seems to me that the best general solution to the dilemma is to distinguish between what could be called "absolute" and "relative" incentives.[13] An absolute incentive is one that makes one's social existence itself into a reward for the right behavior (and that threatens one with loss of social existence for bad behavior). A relative incentive is a reward or punishment that is only relatively desirable or undesirable. Where the basic conditions of one's existence are more or less assured by the community, the positive effects of "grace" can be experienced. One does not have to live in a state of fundamental anxiety. One is encouraged to be a whole person and to relate oneself positively to others. At the same time, judicious use of relative social incentives can help overcome lethargy and steer people away from negative behavior. We want to gain the relative reward or avoid the relative punishment because the first is pleasant and the second is unpleasant. But we do not have to act out of *fundamental* insecurity.

I commend this distinction as the basis for a general social priority in favor of basic security while recognizing that in some instances involving severely antisocial behavior it is sometimes necessary for society to remove its members from normal social interactions altogether. Even so, the aim of rehabilitation should dominate penal policy and nobody should be written out of the human race. (It may be clear from this that I oppose the use of capital punishment, although the issues that poses are beyond the compass of this book.)

These two general priorities are clearly related. Together they suggest that the first order for every community should be to provide the conditions necessary for its members to belong and provide those conditions in such a way that people are secure in their possession.

Before concluding this chapter, I wish to note two corollary points. First, a community must always hold as a high priority its defense from danger, whether human or natural in origin. Little needs to be said here about that, since communities by and large do give this the highest priority. But the way that is done can sometimes pose even larger dangers. For instance, a society can give such a high priority to military defense that it undermines the economic basis for the good life it is supposedly defending. Moreover, the defense can be so threatening to others that the relationships for people of one society are ruptured with those of another. We shall return to this problem in a later chapter. But it should be acknowledged here that protection of the society as a whole is certainly a logical implication of the priority we give to maintaining the conditions necessary for belonging to community.

The other corollary is that a society must provide possibilities for all its members to make creative contributions. What a sociologist might call the role structure of the society is important. Security in one's membership in the society must not be understood passively; it really means that everyone has an active role to play. It also means provision of opportunity for growth in one's creative potentials—so education of all sorts is important, too.

Marking these off as general priorities, we remember that they require active, conscious effort; we cannot expect them to occur as byproducts of a laissez-faire system nor as the contributions of some elite we entrust with the management of society. These are things we have to work together to attain.

CHAPTER FOUR

Economic Realities

When it is said that most of what we see is behind our eyes, the point is not that there isn't anything in front of them. It is that what we see in front of our eyes is filtered and interpreted by the perspective we bring to bear. Such a point must not be overstated. Regardless of our view about it, there *is* an objective world. Our perspective leads us to regard some things as important, others as meaningless. When asked what we see in the real world we are obviously going to center on the things that seem important to us from among the objects that are there to be recorded. And so it is when we come to talk about economic realities. Our perspective leads us to what we consider to be basic. In this chapter, I wish to highlight a number of the most important economic realities of our time, as seen from the standpoint of the ethical perspective discussed in the preceeding chapter. Some of these will be presented as problems, but we are well aware that they might not be viewed as "problems" at all if seen from a different value perspective. In any event, these are dominant economic realities in our time, seen from a Christian orientation.

Vast Expansion of Economic Production

Setting problems of poverty and environment aside for the moment, one is impressed by the enormous expansion of productivity and wealth in recent centuries, an accelerating pace of development showing no signs of abating. If, by means of a time machine, we were able to travel back to the middle of the nineteenth century, we would be astonished, not at what we would see but at what we would *not* see. There would be no automobiles (the roads themselves would be mostly muddy lanes) or airplanes, not to speak of spacecraft. There would be no electric lights or any of the appliances we take for granted that use electric power. There would be no telephones, no radio, no television, no computers and word processors. In the more affluent areas there might be indoor plumbing (that, in fact, goes back to Roman times), but comparatively few people worldwide would have it. There would be no refrigerators, and preservation of food would depend on iceboxes (for the more affluent) or cold cellars on farms or smoking processes. For food one would be dependent pretty largely upon locally grown and preserved items; fresh fruit and vegetables would have to be in season. The infant mortality rates would be high and life expectancy short. A majority of the peole would work long hours on the farm, and those employed in industry would regard a sixty-hour work week as a real luxury. Confronted with illness, one would have to rely on rather primitive cures; many communicable diseases would be fatal. Childbirth would be hazardous. Clothing for the vast majority would be rough-looking. For the wealthy few, clothing would require a good deal of care. One would not see any wash-and-wear fabrics or easy-to-wear mass-produced shoes. And so on.

All that has changed. The pace of change is visible all over the world. Modern forms of communication and transportation and health care and food production are visible almost everywhere (even though we will have to say more about poverty below). Perhaps most remarkably, the world is now able to sustain a population more than three times what it was a century ago (around 1.5 billion people in 1900 to around 4.6 billion in 1984), and with fewer great killer famines or pestilences than a century ago. There are far more people who are "well off" now than there were a century ago, even though (with the great population explosion) there may also be far more people who are destitute. The nuances of such a comparison must be elaborated, of course. But for present purposes, the economic reality is that somehow invention and productivity have enabled many more people to live much better.

Published indices of production bear out the pace of growth. For example, one recently published summary of farm and industrial production from 1960 to 1981 shows substantial increases for every single commodity or kind of product except the harvesting of potatoes (which was down from 314 million short tons in 1960 to 283 million in 1981). Wheat went from 269 million tons to 505 million during that period. Rice production increased from 261 million tons to 456 million; soybeans from 30 million to 97 million; barley from 100 million to 176 million; corn from 226 million to 491 million; fish catches went from 44 million tons to 80 million. Electrical energy production increased from 2,304 billion kWh to 8,134 billion; iron ore from 283 million short tons to 531 million; cement from 349 million to 809 million. The number of motor vehicles produced increased from 16.5 million in 1960 to 37.1 million in 1981.[1] These are aggregate world figures, reflecting vastly greater volume of production and growth in the industrialized countries than in the less developed countries. But even the latter, with all their acknowledged problems, have generally recorded substantial productive growth rates in recent years. Only 12 of 107 countries summarized in the *World Development Report* reported a negative growth rate in Gross National Product per capita. Most showed some growth. China's figure was 5 percent per year; India's was 1.3 percent per year; Pakistan's was 2.8 percent; Indonesia's was 4.2 percent. Even Bangladesh showed a productive growth rate of .3 percent per year.[2] Such figures are of course affected by population growth rates—without those the increases in production would be all the more remarkable. Taken as a whole, the 34 low-income economies recorded an annual per capita growth rate of 3 percent—compared with 3.3 percent per year for the industrial market economies of Europe, North America, and Japan. Such figures are not precise measurements, and they need to be used with caution. But they do make the point that humanity is engaged in a productivity boom of very large proportions.

No doubt some of this is detrimental. For instance, tobacco production went from 4.2 million tons in 1960 to 5.9 million tons in 1978, with the number of cigarettes manufactured increasing from 1,899 billion in 1960 to 3,404 billion in 1978; and environmental effects need to be weighed very carefully. But having registered those cautions, it remains that without substantial production of goods and services human life is not sustainable in the numbers now present on earth. I shall say more about productivity as a priority in a later chapter. For now, let us simply note that there has been a vast expansion in economic production in recent times.

A Widening Gap Between Rich and Poor

The increases in production have not served to bridge the great historic chasm between wealth and poverty. The tendency, both among and within nations, is for the relative gap to increase, even when poor people are improving their lot in absolute terms. Poor people may advance at a rate of 1 or 2 percent per year, while the affluent gain 4 or 5 percent. Even if both gain at the same percentage rate, the gap widens in actual monetary terms. The gap exists within nations and among nations. In the United States, for example, the median family income in 1982 was $20,171. But 9.6 percent of American households had incomes under $5,000 and 8.9 percent were over $50,000—with an even spread between these extremes. Each year the federal government establishes an income level below which persons are officially defined as poor (the level in dollars is adjusted year by year to reflect inflation and increased cost of living). The number of persons below this poverty line decreased substantially during the early 1960s, arriving at a plateau of around 24 to 25 million persons. But the number jumped to 29 million in 1980 and rose to 34.4 million in 1982, of a total population of 231 million.[3] Despite productive expansion in the United States in 1983–85, the number of poor people remained fairly constant. The Bureau of the Census recorded a figure of 33.7 million in late 1985.

Differences become even more dramatic when rich nations and poor nations are contrasted. Thirty-four countries, with a combined population of 2.2 billion, had an annual Gross National Product per capita of $400 or less (with most having less than $300 per capita) in 1982. This included India with $260 per person annual income, Bangladesh with $140, China with $310, and Pakistan with $380. Well over half the world's people live in countries with per-capita GNP of $600 or less. By contrast, 570 million people lived in countries with more than $10,000 in annual Gross National Product per capita in 1982. So here, for example, we have Switzerland at $17,010 and West Germany at $12,460 and the United States at $13,160 compared to China at $310 and India at $260.[4]

In light of the great disparities between the rich and poor nations, it is not surprising that poor countries have begun to complain bitterly and seek changes in basic economic relationships between themselves and the wealthy, industrialized countries. We shall want to discuss this in a later chapter. While recording basic economic realities, however, it is important to note that both rich and poor countries also have wide disparities within themselves. The best-off 10 percent of the population of India, for instance, has 33.6 percent of that nation's income, compared to 7 percent for the lowest 20 percent. Such comparisons are generally even more dramatic if one compares the share of wealth and income held by the top 1 or 2 percent with the lower segments. And the wealthiest people of many Third World countries are substantially richer than middle-income people in prosperous industrialized countries like the United States and West Germany.[5]

Determining the causes of such great disparities of wealth and income in the modern world is very difficult. At least, the easy explanations all seem to cancel each other out! Moreover, it is difficult to assess with any precision just how many people die of starvation each year or are seriously malnourished. But the numbers are very large. There is no denying the basic economic reality that there are rich peole and poor people in this world and that the poor people, vastly more numerous, lack basic necessities.

Widespread Unemployment

Figures on employment and unemployment fluctuate year by year throughout the world. In the industrially developed countries unemployment rates have been unusually high during the late 1970s and early 1980s, reflecting cyclical recession compounded by the shock of oil-price increases and the arrival of the population bulge representing the postwar "baby boom" in the work force. This, in turn, has exacerbated the already high rates of unemployment in developing countries. In the United States and Great Britain, unemployment figures reached their highest levels since the Great Depression of the 1930s. (In the U.S. unemployment reached 9.7 percent in 1982, dropping to 7 percent in 1984 and rising again to 7.3 percent in 1985. In Great Britain unemployment in 1983 was 12.5 percent. In both countries this represented substantial increases, from below 5 percent in the 1960s in the U.S. and from 5.1 percent in the U.K. as recently as 1979.[6] Recession in developed countries diminishes the market for Third World goods which, in turn, increases unemployment in both areas. The unemployment figures for Third World countries are also increased as a natural result of large-scale population growth rates and the inability of relatively small industrial bases to grow rapidly enough to absorb masses of new entrants into the labor market. A sociological byproduct of this situation is the steady stream of young people leaving rural areas where there is no longer enough land to accommodate population increases. These people flock to the cities, swelling their populations far beyond the capacity of their economies to accommodate them or for social services to meet their needs.

Changing cultural patterns also affect unemployment rates. Increasing numbers of women worldwide are seeking jobs in the regular employment market, reflecting changing patterns of family life as well as heightened needs and aspirations of households in all parts of the world. In the more prosperous countries, domestic labor-saving devices reduce the actual workload of homemakers in the home, thereby making it possible for large numbers to seek gainful employment outside the home—a situation that also reflects the decreased actual burden of childrearing in light of more family planning and more universal education and preschool programs removing children from the home for many hours each week. The sudden new entrance of vast numbers of women into the job markets of the world is, in a sense, a one-time thing. Once this has run its course with a large majority of women employed outside the home there will be no similar segment of the population to be absorbed in this way—assuming that most women will in fact wind up in the job market in this way. But the transition period and its effects on current unemployment levels are far from spent.

It is difficult to estimate the effect of increased productivity on jobs. A certain body of literature in the 1960s hailed the far-reaching possibilities of automation and cybernation as promising a new era in which 5 or 10 percent of the population could produce for all the rest.[7] There is some truth in that claim over the long term, since manufacturing is following agriculture in a pattern of diminishing need for production workers. That trend may not be as evident yet in the Third World setting, where full industrial development is still to be achieved. But in most of the industrialized countries new job creation is largely in services, not in traditional industrial work. For example, between 1972 and 1982, while the U.S. economy as a whole was adding some 17 million new jobs, only 446,000 of these were in the traditional blue-collar craft and industrial occupations. The important increases were in services (more than 3 million), clerical work (more than 4 million), sales workers (more than 1 million), management (more than 3 million), and professional and technical work (more than 5 million).[8] Overall, of the 99.5 million jobs existing in 1982, only 21.7 million were in those traditional blue-collar craft and industrial occupations. (Only about 1.5 million workers were engaged in farming.)

Besides illustrating the changing character of the work force, such figures suggest unmistakably that the production of life's necessities no longer has to engage the attention of a majority of the workers in an advanced industrial society. Whether or not 5 or 10 percent of the work force will indeed be able to produce for all the rest in the foreseeable future may be doubtful, but the trend in that direction is now unmistakably clear. In one sense this increased productivity is good news, of course. But it may also mean that unemployment and readjustments in the work force will continue to be serious problems even in the industrialized countries.

Enormous Military Expenditures

In light of the economic development problems and human needs pressing in on most of the world's people, one cannot fail to be impressed by the scale of military expenditures undertaken by many countries. In 1980, 58 leading countries spent more than U.S. $630 billion in this way, almost double the figure for 1971.[9] In the United States alone the military budget for 1980 was $143 billion. That has increased dramatically during the Reagan years to more than $187 billion in 1982 and $258 billion in 1984, with proposed figures reaching beyond the $300 billion level to $446 billion for 1989.[10]

Such figures take on the unreality of most abstractions. But the United States, along with much of the rest of the world, is expending truly monumental sums for military goods and services. What is the economic effect of this? Disarmament enthusiasts sometimes argue that military expenditures are essentially inflationary, on the grounds that military supplies never enter the consumer market although the wages paid to produce them do. By that standard, however, highways, schools, government buildings, and all other public outlays are also inflationary. In fact, military goods and services (along with other public outlays) are bought and sold in the market along with everything else. The purchaser, however, is all the people acting together. Funds are collected from the whole society, through taxation, and then the representatives of the community go into the "market" and order the military supplies. In theory, this works quite as well as any other kind of collective consumption in either the public or private sector. In practice, however, governments sometimes do not collect enough tax money to finance the purchases. The form of the government's borrowing, then, can be either inflationary or recessionary, depending on whether the central bank allows the money supply to increase to accommodate the excess demand. It is widely believed by economists that the Johnson administration's decision not to seek additional taxes to finance the Vietnam War was an important factor in the inflationary tendencies of the late 1960s and the 1970s.

The inflationary or recessionary tendencies of large-scale military spending are important, but they can be offset by technical moves and, in that sense, do not necessarily disrupt an economy. Moreover, even the argument that military spending is economically unsound because it is for things that cannot be consumed represents only a half-truth. That standard would also have to apply to expenditures for many other nonmilitary goods and services that cannot be privately consumed. For that matter, some people doubtless get more psychic pleasure out of the existence of great arsenals in their countries than other people do out of ownership of art objects or jewelry.

But one is still impressed by the fact that these enormous sums of money are being deflected from direct use to deal with the world's obvious needs. It is a startling and even appalling exercise to compare specific military expenditures with specific civilian goods and services. For example, one modern M-1 tank at $2.8 million could buy and equip a good Third World clinic—and 7,071 of those tanks are in the production pipeline in the U.S. at this time of writing. Each of the projected 524 Apache helicopters, at $14 million apiece, could finance more than 10,000 school classrooms in India. One of the projected 26 U.S. cruisers would provide 200,000 Third World orphans complete food, clothing, and medical and educational care from birth through age 20. A Trident submarine's $2 billion cost would finance the building of a rapid transit system for a large city. And so on.

It is not self-evidently true that all military expenditures are wasteful. Certainly most of the residents of London would not have considered the money˜spent on the anti-aircraft guns and fighter planes to have been wasted during the 1940 Battle of Britain. The world is currently a dangerous place. Nonpacifists agree that there are military challenges that have to be met in various military ways if the strong are not to be allowed to take advantage of the more vulnerable. But whatever the need and justification for military defense, it remains true that economic resources poured into armaments are not available for other things. And one cannot help noting the immensity of such expenditures in the presence of so many other needs.

Resource Depletion

Through the 1970s a debate raged over the extent to which humanity was faced with exhaustion of basic resources and environmental pollution. The debate accompanied widespread alarm over runaway population growth rates that were unprecedented in all human history. In itself a tribute to productivity and advances in medicine and nutrition, the population explosion was seen nevertheless to exert new pressures on the world's limited resources. Each new addition to the population is a new producer and a new consumer, and at higher and higher levels of production and consumption, that seemed to spell long-run disaster. One popular book on population referred to each new baby in the advanced countries as a "super-consumer."[11] Publication in 1972 of the First Report to the Club of Rome[12] brought the debate into focus. Based on an elaborate computer model of population growth trends intersecting with trends in production, resource depletion, environmental pollution, etc., the report concluded that continuation of these trends could only spell disaster—a breakdown of the global system. Further writings, such as Jeremy Rifkin's *Entropy,*[13] Robert Heilbroner's *An Inquiry into the Human Prospect,*[14] and the various publications of the Worldwatch Institute[15] further emphasized the dangers.

These writings did not escape judgment. The Club of Rome Report drew chastening technical criticism. The tendency of this and other writings to equate productive progress with increased resource depletion and environmental deterioration was called into question. It was fairly and accurately noted that while advances in production accompanying the Industrial Revolution did entail vast increases in energy consumption and use of raw materials, not infrequently the trend lines of increased efficiency led in the opposite direction. Thus, for example, one could cite how the development of transistors sharply diminished the energy consumption of electronic devices and how automobiles and industrial machines are more efficient than they were a few years ago. It is also frequently argued that inventiveness tends to come into play in time to rescue society when particular resources are about to be depleted. At one time particular kinds of trees were required for the masts of great sailing vessels, and those who had no imagination might have expressed alarm over the depletion of such trees from European forests as the great nations developed their fleets. Such trees today are altogether irrelevant to navigation. Similarly, plastics and other synthetic productions have replaced metals in products of all kinds. The great dependency of industrial civilization on petroleum has led to apprehension over the dwindling of finite oil supplies, deposited by nature over the course of millions of years but used in one great splurge lasting only a few decades or centuries. But it is argued by some that alternative forms of energy will be developed in time to ensure that even the existing limited reserves of petroleum will never all be used. It is also noted that exploration for new oil developments produces more proven reserves each year than the oil that is actually drawn from the ground.

That debate is probably inconclusive as it stands. Fortuitous inventions have occurred, of course, but it is difficult to say that they will necessarily continue to do so. In particular, the historical dependency of the Industrial Revolution on fossil fuels (first coal, then petroleum) makes the indisputably limited reserves of such fuels a matter of very great economic consequence. It apparently took the shock of high petroleum prices in the 1970s to bring that point home. And while it may be that the scurrying around to develop alternative and virtually limitless forms of energy—such as solar or nuclear fusion—will be successful, it must be admitted that the big breakthroughs have not yet occurred. Until they do, the fate of the whole vast industrial development of the world, and the greatly enlarged world population, is hostage to a yet-uncertain future.

This may be even more true when one considers environmental damage resulting from the stresses of industrial civilization. It may be a fact, as Milton and Rose Friedman assert, that "the air is cleaner and the water safer today than one hundred years ago" and "the air is cleaner and the water safer in the advanced countries of the world today than in the backward countries."[16] But if one takes the whole of a country like the United States the judgment about the air is questionable, and if one compares either air or water in the "backward" countries today with those same countries 100 years ago, deterioration has undoubtedly occurred. (The cleanup of both air and water in the industrialized countries also owes much more to public outrage and governmental action than the Friedmans would willingly concede!) In any event, industrialized civilization has had indisputably negative effects, whether or not the community has found it possible to overcome many of them. The economic reality is that the great benefits derived from increased productivity have not been without costs, even though the benefits have sometimes been easier to measure (in market terms) than the costs.

There is the further question whether the immense scale of industrial expansion worldwide may bring on universal catastrophes of unforeseeable dimensions. For example, will drastic climatic changes occur resulting from the depletion of the ozone layer of the upper atmosphere? Will "acid rain" destroy the biological balance irreversibly in the world's rivers, lakes, and oceans? Will thermal pollution melt the polar icecaps, raising ocean levels and flooding the great coastal plains on which much of the world's population and much of its agricultural and industrial production is to be found? (Or, alternatively, will there be a new ice age with opposite but equally ominous dangers?) Will nuclear war make the planet uninhabitable for anything but cockroaches?

I do not know the answers to such questions—and who really does? But the fact that such questions can be raised is to point toward a level of economic reality that is too often segregated from other economic discussions.

World Economics and National Boundaries

Most discussions of economic policy are conducted at the national level. But tensions of various kinds are now being experienced between an increasingly worldwide economic order and the primarily national form of political organization. For example, it is generally believed that governments can stimulate economic activity during a recession by increasing demand. This can be done by some combination of monetary policies designed to increase the supply of money and fiscal policies increasing direct governmental spending or lowering taxes, either of which serves to increase purchasing power. More goods are then purchased and ordered, and in the enlarged market business people are encouraged to expand their facilities, jobs are created, the economy grows. On the other hand, it is generally believed that governments can reverse this when excessive demand generates inflation. The money supply can be constricted, governmental spending curtailed, and taxes increased. Half the fun of contemporary economic forecasting and advising of politicians is to determine exactly which mix of these possibilities is desirable.

But it remains true that the international dimension can frustrate the best-laid plans of either economists or politicians. For example, one of the "supply-side" policies of the Reagan administration was to grant substantial tax reductions, concentrating them in the "investing classes," on the assumption that this would lead to greater savings and capital investment. If that tactic were attempted in dozens of countries one could name, the effect would either be to increase direct consumption or to encourage investment *outside* the country involved. The policy did not in fact work quite as intended even in the United States, where some of the additional money was used for increased consumption and for the acquisition of already existing enterprises. Currently hundreds of billions of U.S. dollars are being held abroad and hundreds of billions of dollars are held in the U.S. by foreign investors, such as Arabs with their large oil revenues. Abrupt decisions by foreigners to withdraw their funds or to spend them for U.S. goods would have massive effects on U.S. economic stability that would be largely beyond the control of the U.S. government or central bank.

Much has been written in recent years about the dramatic increase in size and influence of transnational corporations. These major companies are principally based in one country but have substantial involvements in other countries, both in manufacturing and in sales. Adroit maneuvering of production, sales, and accounting among the far-flung units of such corporations makes it possible to exploit the most favorable tax and labor environments and to avoid the attempts by any one government to control them. The point should not be overstated, because major transnational corporations can be quite vulnerable to political pressures within even a small country. But the point still expresses important economic realities.

Currently there is a good deal of discussion in the United States of the "runaway jobs" phenomenon. The character of modern production is such that many operations can be transferred to poor Third World countries where unskilled or semiskilled labor can be performed for wages substantially below those required by union contracts or minimum wage laws in the U.S. Unemployment in the U.S. resulting in part from this exporting of jobs puts pressure on the U.S. labor force as a whole to accept lower wages. The world scale of economic activity thereby makes it difficult for this or any other individual nation to determine its own labor policies.

Similar things could be said about attempts to control unethical policies of major corporate enterprises. Such enterprises are forced to compete globally, which means they are vulnerable to the competition of firms cutting corners in all directions. When the government of Liberia attempted in the early 1980s to require the extensive Firestone Rubber operations in that country to improve social benefits to its workers, it was informed by the company that that would be quite impossible—and the implication was left that the company might have to transfer its operations elsewhere. Indeed, the company is involved in a competitive industry and for it to increase its labor costs substantially in Liberia would possibly make it more vulnerable to other firms with lower labor costs elsewhere. Of course, the fact that Firestone conducts operations in Liberia at low wages and with only modest social benefits also means that other companies have to compete with *that* standard! And when, after a worldwide campaign and the pressure of a major boycott, the Nestlé Company accepted responsibility for the marketing of infant-formula products in such a way that mothers not needing the product would not be induced to buy it, that company made itself vulnerable to marketing competition by a number of other companies not operating under similar ethical restraints. Any one country, confronting problems of this kind, could adopt regulations binding on all market participants—and, indeed, a number of countries have moved to do so. But the global industry as such does not operate under a global regime.

Illustrations of various kinds could be added to suggest that economic life is increasingly global in its scope, and yet social controls still have to be mounted at the national level.

Potentialities and Frustrations

Much more would have to be written to convey a fully rounded picture of the dominant economic realities of our time. There is room for considerable debate as to *why* some of these realities are as they are even before we entered into the question of what should be done. But from this sketch there emerges one point of surpassing importance: The world has at its disposal unprecedented potential for dealing fundamentally with human need and for ensuring the future of the common human enterprise. Industrial productivity and technological inventiveness are at a peak without historical precedent; the possibilities for our economic future seem virtually limitless. The capacity is at hand for feeding, clothing, sheltering, and providing health care for all the world's people, and the means are available for progressively liberating humanity from the more burdensome forms of toil and for providing educational and cultural enrichment heretofore limited only to elite classes.

At the same time, however, this great potentiality gives rise to an equally great sense of frustration that we have not been able to do these things *directly.* This must be due in part to sheer human selfishness and shortsightedness, fostered by unnecessarily competitive attitudes toward economic life. But in part it must also be because it has not been considered *possible* economically for society to act directly to order its priorities and achieve its economic and social goals.

Attitudes toward the feasibility of direct management of the economy for social ends parallel, in part, the commitments we have to "capitalism" or "socialism." But does humanity have to await the resolution of that historic controversy before assuming responsibility for its collective destiny? A largely capitalist economy can still be used deliberately and creatively by a democratic government to facilitate social ends, just as a largely socialist economy can make creative use of the market mechanism. In the chapters that follow, we shall examine several areas of social priority more closely—not with a precommitment to either "capitalism" or "socialism," but with a recognition that society can use government wisely or unwisely under either system.

CHAPTER FIVE

Priority One: Adequate Production

> *Intellectual critics of capitalism have been eager to point to the negative aspects of economic rationality and to ignore its positive effects: efficiency and growth. . . . But though there is no unambiguous case for economic efficiency and growth, there is certainly an ambiguously positive one. For is not the first task of an economic order to economize, to be as efficiently productive as possible? Its job is to produce the wealth which provides the possibility for civilization in its material and a good deal of its nonmaterial aspects.*
>
> —Robert Benne (1981)[1]

> *It is one of the most basic of contemporary socialist truths that the good society only becomes possible when there is a technology of abundance and a mass movement capable of mastering it. . . . (Socialism) is a possibility based upon the unprecedented development of technology and it can become an actuality only when there is a conscious majority that masters that productivity and puts it to the service of human need.*
>
> —Michael Harrington (1972)[2]

There is apparent agreement between a committed capitalist and a committed socialist at a basic point: The no. 1 priority of economic life must be productivity. Benne here joins Michael Novak, George Gilder, and virtually all advocates of capitalism in asserting that the production of wealth is finally what economic life is all about. Without it, nothing else is possible. Poverty, Novak will declare, requires no explanation. That is the natural state of humankind and has been from the beginning. It is wealth that requires explanation, and the explanation that most capitalist thinkers offer for the development of wealth and well-being is, not surprisingly, capitalism. Some capitalist thinkers, such as Joseph Schumpeter, even argue that the capitalist development of wealth is egalitarian in tendency: mass production becomes production for the masses.[3] The engine of private wealth accumulation presses us toward the development of mass markets and the production of an ever-enlarging cornucopia of goods for the general run of people. Other capitalist thinkers are at least bound to assert that the poorest elements of the population will find their lives improving as benefits trickle down to them from the growing prosperity of the well-to-do.

A socialist like Michael Harrington is skeptical about that; but he, too, regards production as the sine qua non of social well-being. It is even the precondition for socialism because, as he is quick to say, you cannot socialize poverty.[4] (That is, incidentally, his chief criticism of some forms of Third World socialism.) Socialism becomes a possibility after certain levels of technology have developed and after a movement comes into being that is capable of asserting both political and technical mastery over it.

Is This the Highest Priority?

So, with socialist and capitalist voices both speaking of technology and production as a high priority, who is to disagree? Certainly there are some who would at least raise serious questions about the negative environmental effects of too much of the wrong kind of technological development, and not all of the goods produced by technology are unmixed blessings. But putting such points aside for the moment, we can perhaps agree that there is need for a material base of goods and services without which everything else is endangered.

That point is underscored theologically by the mainstream of Hebrew and Christian teaching about creation. The created world is good, and we as part of creation are dependent on the meeting of physical needs. Without food, clothing, shelter, etc., we perish. Even when we have enough to stay alive, the struggle for marginal subsistence can be so severe that all other aspects of our humanity are crowded out. Profound physical insecurity can undermine the overall sense of security on which our receptivity to God's grace often practically depends—as we must eat, as it were, the bread of anxious toil. And even if basic physical security can be assured through an adequate base of production, there is still the question whether we are going on to enrich existence with facilities enhancing our creativity and community life. Humanity does not require symphony orchestras. Jesus and St. Paul, Plato and Moses never heard one, although they could

experience other forms of music. But still, Bach and Beethoven and
Mahler have greatly enriched the human condition, each in his own way
deepening our esthetic grasp of the wonder of God's creation and gracious
love. If that is so, one must agree that the somewhat humbler but no less
necessary inventors and artisans who have brought the various orchestral
instruments into being have served this same cause. And then too, for the
sake of those who live in areas remote from the great symphony orchestras, is it not a similar enrichment of the esthetic dimension of human life
that inventors and producers have brought magnificent performances into
individual homes through stereo sets?

Could one not similarly argue that it is a good and remarkable thing
that modern forms of communication and transportation have so linked
together scattered parts of this vast world that we can more directly experience both our common humanity and our incredible diversity? That, too,
bespeaks a high degree of productive achievement. During the years when
environmental alarmism was at its peak (and, make no mistake, there has
been much to be alarmed about in the ecological threats accompanying all
this productive development), one was often enough treated to the specta-
cle of speakers rushing from place to place by jet aircraft to present their
largely antitechnological message.[5] One does not have to endorse all technological developments, however, to appreciate that many of them have
greatly enriched the common life. One may suppose theologically that this
is in the direction of the fulfillment of God's purposes for creative human
existence on earth.

Is production, then, the *highest* priority? There may be a sense in which
that is so. But the point needs to be made cautiously, because the material
realm is still primarily to be understood as instrumental to other things.
The same Jesus who taught that we should pray for "our daily bread"
also said that we do not live "by bread alone." One shorthand way to
express this is to say that economic production is a necessary condition to
every other priority but that it is not a sufficient condition. It is a necessary base for everything else. But providing that base does not *guarantee*
anything else. Production can, in fact, be undertaken in such a way that
other important priorities are undermined. I have the impression that some
technological enthusiasts believe we need only keep economic growth
booming along to assure all other worthwhile human good. If so, that may
owe much to the nineteenth-century marriage of some capitalist thought
with the utilitarian identification of material pleasure with good. It can be
assumed, and has been, that the more material consumption we provide
for through productive growth, the happier we will all be. But that is very
far from being the truth.

So this foundational priority remains basic; but it cannot be treated as "first" or "highest" in the sense that it best expresses the meaning of human existence or that it necessarily leads to the epitome of human fulfillment. And that way of stating the matter means that we cannot avoid more careful consideration of *what* is to be produced and *how* it is to be produced and *for whom* it is to be produced. Giving high priority to material production, as we must, does not excuse us from serious thought about other priorities or from considering how other priorities affect the way we approach production itself.

The Organization of Production

The capitalist thinkers referred to in the beginning of this chapter obviously believe that capitalism offers the best, if not the only, way to assure adequate production. Harrington and other socialist thinkers clearly do not agree with that, although socialists from Marx onward have given capitalism credit for laying the foundations for the miracles of large-scale productive enterprise. I am not sure the dispute between capitalists and socialists on this point can yet be resolved. Certainly capitalism has played a very important role in the Industrial Revolution. And there are socialists who seem willing to concede that socialism has not yet learned how to solve the production problem—at least not adequately. But there is plenty of evidence that production *can* occur successfully under state auspices just as that it can be stimulated by a private enterprise system. The Soviet Union, though plagued by great economic difficulties including insufficient production of food in recent years, still seems to have the second largest Gross National Product in the world.[6] Other socialist countries present a mixture of evidence regarding productivity. All have problems, but few are to be numbered among the poorest countries and some, such as Czechoslovakia and the German Democratic Republic, have very strong records of productive growth.

The reason for noting this comparison, however, is not to try to settle the capitalism-vs.-socialism debate but to say that there is no reason why we have to be dogmatic about how society should meet its production priorities.

In many countries, agricultural production is a particularly sensitive point. It is often alleged in Western capitalist countries that the effort to collectivize farming in the Soviet Union and other socialist countries has proved disastrous. Indeed, a number of socialist countries, including the Soviet Union, have confirmed this judgment at least to the extent of having to provide some latitude for a parallel private sector where individual farmers can market a part of their produce directly to the consumers. One of the interesting features of downtown Bucharest, for instance, is a large open farmer's market where peasants bring their produce for sale, often sleeping there on the spot through the night. The point seems to be that when traditional farming is collectivized it destroys the incentive of farmers or peasants to spend those extra long hours lavishing attention on crops and lifestock to increase production. Partly for this reason, the Sandinista government in Nicaragua chose not to undertake a radical land-reform program or to collectivize agriculture in general in areas where existing farming was highly productive. Maximization of agricultural production was simply held to be a higher priority than other objectives of the revolution: First the people had to be fed and export crops had to be protected for the sake of foreign exchange earnings badly needed by the country for other purposes. Many years earlier, the Soviet Union had arrived at the same conclusion through its New Economic Program (1921), although that compromise with capitalism was ended essentially with the first five-year plan of 1928.

Capitalist countries have similarly been willing to sacrifice the purity of their laissez-faire principles for the sake of maintaining or increasing production. Extraordinary moves in both the United States and the United Kingdom to save the Chrysler Company's automobile production violated the normal canon that inefficient firms should be permitted to collapse so the factors of production they control can be released for more efficient uses. Farm-subsidy programs in the United States have served to protect farm production during periods when depressed market conditions threaten agricultural instability.

With all their problems, neither the United States nor the Soviet Union is in any danger of serious economic hardship due to lost production of vital commodities. But one does not have to look very far in the contemporary world to find exactly that situation. Many Third World countries are having to mortgage their futures in order to import food and other critically needed commodities. Often this is in the face of underutilized land and a high unemployment rate. In many Third World countries policies have not served to maximize agricultural production, and the effect has weakened the economy as a whole. In Ghana, for example, many of the most talented young people have fled the countryside in search of more desirable living circumstances in the cities of that and neighboring countries. Moreover, the infrastructure of highways and transport facilities has lagged, so that existing produce is sometimes difficult to get to markets. High priority for agricultural production in such a setting would somehow have to make the rural areas more attractive socially while also accelerating the pace of road development. (This kind of problem is currently more typical of Africa than of Asia, for in Asia most arable land is already under intensive cultivation.) China has almost miraculously succeeded in feeding itself in recent decades, believing for a long time that this could only be done through oppressive measures to keep people in their appointed places in rural communes—a policy now being relaxed with generally favorable results.

My main point here is not to extol any particular form of organization or production, but rather to say that basic production had better be given high priority and that whatever kind of organization clearly seems necessary to that end had better be used unless it is in itself utterly dehumanizing.

What Is to Be Produced?

The possible trade-offs between the priorities of production and other social and political priorities force us to look more closely at *what* is being produced. It is one thing to speak of the absolute necessity of adequate agricultural production, and to give this priority over almost everything else. It is quite another to give the production of luxury goods higher priority than personal and social values. If one could easily mark off the line between necessity and luxury one might deal with the priorities question something like this: (1) the production of necessities should normally be given priority over everything else, while (2) other priorities reflecting the essential nature and purpose of human life should be given priority over the production of luxuries wherever the two conflict.

Regrettably, the line cannot always be drawn so easily. Some things (like books of poetry or pianos) which are luxuries from a purely physical standpoint may themselves be important to the fulfillment of some of the priorities reflecting the essential nature of human life. Socially and culturally speaking (and we *are*, after all, social and cultural beings), what is "necessary" to one person may be a "luxury" to another, and vice versa. Strictly speaking, a child can be warmly and comfortably clothed with pink trousers, a green and purple shirt, a brown coat that is two sizes too large, and two shoes of the same size but of different style and color. But in most school settings around the world, such a get-up would be a social disaster! Warm and comfortable clothing that is also reasonably representative of current style may well be a social necessity, particularly for children. So adequate production has a cultural as well as physical dimension.

In the complexities of contemporary economic life there is also another complication. One group of people may have to produce luxuries for another group in order to receive bare necessities in return. That is, in fact, a routine phenomenon in societies where luxury goods exist at all. Those who are employed making or building them receive wages that they, in turn, use to buy the necessities of life. Few employees of the Rolls Royce

Company actually own Rolls Royce automobiles. But those who buy those luxury cars provide the money used by Rolls Royce employees for the purchase of essential food, clothing, and shelter—a fact that no doubt mitigates whatever resentment those employees may have at having to make things they could never own for themselves.

This relationship may be even more important internationally. First World countries provide a market for Third World goods. This means that Third World people make things—things that may well be luxuries—that are then exchanged for goods produced in the First World, goods that may well be necessities. We must postpone for a time considering the distortions often appearing in such relationships to note that this is why recession in the rich countries spreads so quickly to poor ones. When there is high unemployment in North America and Europe, fewer people in the rich countries there can afford to buy the commodities and products of poor countries—and that, in turn, causes unemployment and deeper poverty in those countries so their people cannot afford to buy necessities. I am oversimplifying this kind of relationship, of course. But there is enough reality in it to mean that sometimes the production of luxuries for some is almost a precondition of the production of necessities for others. And in general one can observe that the overall economic stimulation (and differentiation of production) afforded by production of things that are not strictly necessary may be very helpful in generating the production of things that are.

So it is not always easy to give high priority to the production of some things without also giving high priority to others. Still, the distinction between necessity and luxury is important when social priorities are established. The production of luxuries should at least have to bear the burden of proof when it seems to stand in the way of our meeting other goals of greater importance.

A further distinction is routinely made in all discussion of economics, one not very well understood by lay persons. That is the distinction between production of capital goods and goods for consumption. Capital goods are the things that are needed for the production of the things we consume directly: production machinery, freight transportation facilities, manufacturing plants, electrical power generators, etc. No matter what form of exchange an economy practices, it must invest a certain portion of its resources in capital goods. A growing economy generally invests a great deal in such goods. The fact that less than 3 percent of the work force in the United States is now able to grow the crops needed to feed the whole country (and a substantial part of the rest of the world as well) is not just a tribute to the increased dedication and energy of farmers! If anything, the 3 percent probably expend less energy than the 50 percent who were needed to feed a much smaller population in the year 1900. It is the revolution in farm machinery, fertilizers, and hybrid grains that accounts for the vast increase in farm productivity.

A certain amount of misplaced moral rhetoric attacks "wealth" and "profits" without paying close enough attention to the relationship between capital goods and consumer goods. The popular conception of wealth emphasizes the latter more than the former. We think of a wealthy person as one who has a large supply of money and who owns luxurious houses, automobiles, clothes, jewelry, yachts, etc. But wealth also refers to the ownership of the factors of production, and such things as land and capital goods may not so readily translate into personal consumption. Under normal conditions, stock in great corporations can be sold and the proceeds used for personal consumption. But if all of the owners of capital goods tried to do this at once they would quickly learn that there were not enough buyers. Most of the wealth of a great nation is tied up in its productive capacity—and that cannot be consumed directly. There are, to be sure, moral issues involved in the ownership of a society's productive capacity; but these issues have more to do with power than with consumption per se. There certainly are differences in purchasing power that closely parallel the ownership of productive capacity. But "wealth" in the sense of a large and growing accumulation of capital goods is important to a society regardless of the form of ownership.

Similarly, "profits" have a negative connotation among people who think of this as an unearned reward derived from the sweat and labor of others. But again, no society could simply return all the fruits of the labor of its workers to the workers themselves without neglecting the needed production of capital goods. Insofar as "profits" simply represent this margin of difference between those things that are returned to workers for consumption and what is invested in further production itself, it is necessary for economic growth. There is room for considerable debate as to who should receive this margin—that is, who should control decisions about investment, etc.—but the existence of some margin of profit is necessary.

Part of the rub, however, is in the fact that resources devoted to the production of capital goods almost necessarily represent deferred consumption. This is likely to be a good bargain in the long run, since the capital goods will increase productivity and result in an overall growth in the supply of consumer goods. That is in the long run. But in the short run it may mean that the supply of consumer goods will be less than it might have been had that received full attention. Historically, in one after another of the countries going through the transition into the Industrial Revolution, the difference between the long run and the short run has been one or two generations. In countries as diverse as England and the Soviet Union, one or two generations of workers had to suffer while waiting for the fruits of industrial development to be achieved. Not uncommonly, the very first generation of industrial workers has been worse off than its parents were back on the farm. One of the serious questions confronting underdeveloped countries today is how to go through this transition without forcing ordinary people to sacrifice too much.

In a number of countries, for instance, a hot debate rages over whether social programs should be cut back drastically in order to improve the balance of payments. Countries like Brazil, Argentina, and Mexico—to name only three relatively strong Third World economies—are under considerable pressure from the International Monetary Fund to curtail expansive social programs as a condition of receiving help in meeting interest payments on existing international loans. In effect, such countries are being asked to devote more resources directly to the capital development process, resources that then would be unavailable for consumption through social programs.[7]

So here is a classic dilemma requiring the most rigorous examination of conflicting priorities. The dilemma is made all the more difficult because governments confront the most intensive counterpressures from their own people. What is almost necessary from an economic standpoint may be almost impossible politically.

It is possible, of course, for an underdeveloped country or region to receive capital assistance from a more prosperous society so that the accumulation of such resources does not have to come directly out of the labor and deferred consumption of poor people. That is an option that was unavailable to the first countries making the industrial transition. But even now, capital transfers from rich to poor countries require deferred consumption by somebody. Direct grants from wealthy countries mean that some consumption by the people of those countries must be forgone or at least postponed. But the people of wealthy countries are much less likely to feel the pinch. More will be said about this below. For now, we will simply note that the decision on the proper balance in production between capital and consumer goods is a very important one. Clearly, if production itself is deserving of high priority, then capital investment must be supported as a means to that end.

The Production Priority and Other Priorities

While productivity itself is very important, we have noted that it cannot stand by itself. Without adequate production all other economic and social objectives are likely to fall short. But we still are forced again and again to make decisions about how we are to go about fostering production. Shall we reply primarily on the free-market mechanism or on the public sector? What shall we produce? How are we to distinguish between necessities and luxuries, and is it true that luxuries for some are prerequisite to the production of necessities for others? What shall be the mix between capital goods and consumer goods—and how shall we allocate the sacrifices necessary for the accumulation of a sufficient industrial base? Is it morally justifiable to sacrifice the basic well-being of a whole generation or two in order to make a livable existence possible for all subsequent generations—if such a tragic decision really has to be made?

The fact that such dilemmas must be faced means that we cannot designate productivity as our first priority in any simple way. We cannot say, for instance, that we will deal with productivity as such first and only after that is secure turn our attention to other priorities. The point is that other kinds of priority-setting affect the *way* we address the foundational problem of ensuring enough production to meet the needs of society. Priority-setting as it relates to economic life is not, therefore, a "lexical" ordering of objectives.[8] It is necessary to have some sense of all the important priorities and of how they relate to one another and define one another.

As we turn, then, to four other kinds of priorities we will expect further illumination concerning the issues that have been opened up in relation to the first priority, that of economic production.

CHAPTER SIX

Priority Two: Equity and Security

> . . . *equality, the final goal of the social art!*
> —Condorcet (1793?)

> *Some people are better than others. They deserve more of society's rewards, of which money is only one small part. A principal function of social policy is to make sure they have the opportunity to reap those rewards.*
> —Charles Murray (1984)[1]

Do differences of wealth and income matter? In chapter 4 we reviewed some current data about such differences. It is more difficult to see this in human terms, but we must try. One of the main theses of Michael Harrington's book *The Other America*[2] was that poverty in the United States is often hidden from the sight of people who are not poor. He was able to point to the squalid ghettoes of large cities, the rural outbacks of Appalachia and Indian reservations, the solitary existence of the elderly poor. It is possible to live a normal middle-class existence in the United States without experiencing any of this. One is simply not aware of the existence of people who are actually poor.

If that was true of the America of the 1960s, it is no less true on a world scale in the 1980s. Rich people in Third World countries can scarcely evade this reality—walls surrounding their homes topped by broken glass embedded in concrete bear witness to a recognition that theirs is a privileged existence. But North Americans, Europeans, Japanese, and Australians do not have to confront this reality so directly. Perhaps it would matter to them if they did; perhaps it would not.

How might the affluent respond, for example, to Mathare Valley? Mathare Valley is a vast slum, located in a dried river valley on the outskirts of Nairobi, Kenya. Most of the 100,000 people who dwell there are economic and social refugees from rural Kenya: a family that is no longer able to make it on the land, a young unwed mother who has been ostracized by her community, others who are just down on their luck. This vast throng of poor people is huddled together in shacks so tightly packed that one could almost walk across the valley on the rusty tin and plastic roofs if they were solid enough to support one's weight. Here the little children share disease germs in utterly unsanitary conditions, and there is never enough food. Water is piped through by the city—which is fortunate by Third World slum standards—but it must be bought by the inhabitants, as must the wood or charcoal used for cooking. A small clinic and job training center, where mothers learn how to care for their babies and eke out a meager income through sewing, is to be found on the edge of the valley. It is one of a handful of such institutions, reaching a fragment of the population with a fragment of hope and opportunity. Staff members of such centers quickly suffer burnout if they allow themselves to be sensitive to the human condition. It is possible for other people never to know.

Or there is Agua de Dios (literally, "water of God"), a town at the base of the Colombian Andes. Originally a leper colony, Agua de Dios still houses a couple thousand elderly lepers in attractive but hardly luxurious facilities (one rarely sees younger lepers since the disease can now be treated successfully). Elsewhere in the town one finds large numbers of schoolchildren for whom the one decent meal a day is provided by a program sponsored by the Catholic relief agency CARITAS. There are few automobiles or social amenities in Agua de Dios. There are a very caring church and devoted teachers for the children, and there is the feeding program, and there is a small clinic where malnutrition is one of the most typical diagnoses made by the overworked staff. Housing is poor, reflecting the poverty of most of the people.

Or there is the refugee camp in San Vicente, El Salvador. Residents there are mainly refugees from war. Most have been there two or three years. Asked why they are there, many will reply "por causa de miedo" (literally, "because of fear"). The 10,000 or so residents live hand to mouth on a combination of small food allocations from relief agencies and income derived from marginal work opportunities in the area. Ten or a dozen men, women, and children may be huddled in a single room in the long row of housing units constructed of adobe bricks. Cooking is done in an open porch setting in front. Sanitary facilities consist of squalid-looking "outhouses." The mortality rate is not unusually high because of periodic visits by health personnel, but the swarms of children appear to be chronically unhealthy.

The interesting thing about these three settings is that they are far from being the poorest in the world. None is quite as bad from a nutritional standpoint as parts of the Sahel, or the vast, teeming slums of Bombay or Calcutta, or parts of Haiti or Bolivia or Bangladesh. None is as bad as the images of Ethiopia visible on television screens in Western countries in 1984–85. Still, a George Gilder might feel that these people are getting full measure of what poor people need most of all in order to succeed: "the spur of their poverty."[3] The rest of us, confronting the reality as best we can, are left to ponder the question of the meaning of such poverty. Surely it has practical aspects that cannot be neglected. But prior to all practical questions is the theological one: Does it matter? And if so, why?

Theological Considerations

What really *is* at stake in the vast differences of income and wealth one can observe throughout the world today? Some of the theological points raised in chapter 3 speak to this.

Most obviously, of course, is the sheer reality of physical suffering. Physical health and well-being are basic to almost everything else, given the way God has created this world. If God's purposes through creation are not to be frustrated, a basic, rudimentary minimum of physical well-being has to be reached for everybody. Whatever the cause of the poverty in places like Mathare Valley and Agua de Dios, it is a problem in the most exact sense of that word. It is a point of tension between reality as it is and reality as God created it to be. Malnourished, diseased children suffer, and they are not able to grow up to be all that they otherwise might be. Their God-given potentialities remain locked in the vault of human circumstance. Some die before their time. Most grow up only equipped to perpetuate cycles of poverty and frustration. From a sheer physical standpoint, the meaning of the doctrine of creation is on the line here. For we must ask, was God's act of creation for *this?*

But poverty is relational as well as physical. Sometimes it is said that poverty in the United States and Europe is not a serious matter because poor people in these affluent settings are themselves affluent by world standards. We must grant some truth to that. The urban ghettoes and the rural slums remain. But few of these places can match the depth of destitution achieved by Mathare Valley, not to speak of Ethiopia or Bangladesh. But the theological perspective requires us to confront not only the realities of physical suffering but also the relational effects of the gulf between wealth and poverty. For we are made to belong to one another in the life of community, and whatever frustrates that intention is also a theological problem.

Earlier we suggested as a first general priority that it should be possible for everyone to be able to function as a member of the community. We all need to have a sense of belonging. We all need to be accepted by others, to be able to interact at a fully human level with others, to participate responsibly with others in the common life. From this perspective it should be apparent that poverty is a relational condition, and not just a physical reality. The two aspects of poverty—the physical and the relational—are both theologically important. But they raise different kinds of questions. The problem of physical deprivation translates into suffering and lost potentialities. But relational poverty translates into broken relationships, unfulfilled community, loss of self-esteem on one side and inflated pride on the other. Physical poverty represents a frustration of the intentions of creation; relational poverty undermines the purpose and possibilities of covenant. The two reinforce each other, but they are also different. It is possible to have either one without the other. In a society in which all are physically poor but where there are no great inequalities, there can be great suffering and loss of possibilities. But there may still be a deep sense of community—even a kind of fellow feeling in the presence of misery. On the other hand, in a society in which there is none of this deep physical deprivation but where there are great inequalities, there may be no physical suffering but at the same time there may be little sense of mutuality in community.

We must remind ourselves that the fulfillment of human potentialities and the realization of community never automatically follow from any economic arrangement. Equality does not guarantee mutuality. Physical well-being does not assure the fulfillment of possibilities. The best economic situation is, at best, but a precondition for the flowering of our humanity under God. And the worst situation is but an obstacle, although it may be an insurmountable one. Bonded together in love, a family or a community can confront great hardship together while yet another family or community is torn apart by division in spite of material prosperity. The best of all worlds is when there is material sufficiency shared in such a way that our humanity is enhanced. But the point I wish to emphasize here is that a theological perspective on this does not allow us to neglect *either* the meeting of physical needs *or* the effect of economic arrangements on the quality of community life. Both are important.

But one side or the other can easily be lost in the debate over economic justice. On the one hand, it is possible to be so caught up in the quest for liberation from oppression that one forgets the oppressiveness of want itself. On the other hand, it is possible to so emphasize material well-being that one forgets how economics affects relationships.

Note, for example, the way the influential philosopher John Rawls has framed the question. Rawls clearly regards poverty as a serious moral problem, to the point that he defines justice from the standpoint of what the poorest, least privileged members of society would consider to be in their interest. Equality is the norm of justice, and the only acceptable inequalities are the ones that the least privileged would themselves consider to be in their own interest. What might these be? Clearly they would not include inequalities that benefit only the rich—"trickle-down" economics that never quite trickles down. But they might include inequalities that are necessary to generate greater production so long as the poor are also better off in the long run. As Rawls puts it, "there is no injustice in the greater benefits earned by a few provided that the situation of persons not so fortunate is thereby improved."[4] Perhaps it takes a good deal of incentive to generate production, and incentives by definition lead to inequalities. Poor people as well as rich people need the production. And as long as they are better off as a result of the increased production, poor people can therefore agree that the inequalities are an expression of justice. As far as it goes, the logic is compelling. The same general point is registered by Arthur M. Okun's thoughtful monograph *Equality and Efficiency: The Big Tradeoff.*[5] Okun acknowledges the ethical case for equality but argues at the same time that equality is opposed to productive efficiency: "Although the ethical case for capitalism is totally unpersuasive, the efficiency case is thoroughly compelling to me."[6] Philosophers like Rawls and economists like Okun take the plight of the poor seriously, but they are persuaded that the poor are also benefited by inequality insofar as inequality is needed for productive efficiency.

As well the poor may be. But what one finds missing from such an analysis is recognition that well-being cannot be defined exclusively in material terms. No doubt there is a kind of material threshold below which the quality of relationships is altogether secondary to the meeting of rudimentary human needs. But above that level one cannot argue in any simple way that every increase in *material* benefits, by itself, necessarily improves the well-being of the poor. It is a question of when one really is "better off." Rawls and Okun, along with many other writers, tend to assume a material definition of the term rather than a relational one. It is as though life were basically a competitive game in which one's interest were necessarily pitted against the interests of others. Justice and "fairness" are on the side of equality in that game except insofar as the least privileged participants find otherwise in their own interest. But interest is then defined in very individual and material terms.

While acknowledging that this perspective does at least take the plight of the poor very seriously, a theological perspective (or, for that matter, a thoughtfully humanistic one) must insist on a more social, relational understanding of what "better off" really means. The relational cost of productive efficiency may come too high if the result is a fragmented common life in which self-centeredness is the last moral word.

Indeed, a good deal of the material incentive built into most present economic systems—socialist as well as capitalist—may be as much social as material. That is, the incentive may be to improve one's social standing or at least to prevent it from deteriorating. The economist Fred Hirsch makes this point obliquely through his distinction between the material economy and the positional economy.[7] The positional economy involves goods, services, etc., that are inherently scarce or subject to "congestion" or "crowding" the more they are used. Positional goods cannot be made more abundant to accommodate increased demand. In a strict sense, the more one person has, the less another can have. The consumption of positional goods therefore does more than fill a need or provide a pleasurable luxury: it defines one's place in society. It marks whether one is above or below others. According to Hirsch, the existence of a positional economy establishes social limits to economic growth. All the growth in the world will not overcome the positional scarcity. The only question is where one stands in the economic hierarchy defined by consumption of positional goods.

Insofar as economic motivation is made to center around improving one's social standing, it appears to run directly counter to love. Such motivation means that one is "better" or "worse" than somebody else, whether one is able to dominate others or be dominated by them, whether one is in a position to receive recognition from others based on one's standing. If a theological understanding of love is founded on God's unmerited grace and the expression of kinship and mutuality with others, it would appear that positional motivation runs directly counter to the faith. It would appear that "first prize" in the great economic contest is, ironically, to be more deeply separated from others—which is last prize theologically. We can only "win" by losing something of our humanity.

We may be so locked into self-centeredness and "original sin" that such motivations must be appealed to in order to create the necessary levels of production without which serious physical deprivation and suffering occur. Such motivation may be a lesser evil. But even if it is, one should never define justice in terms that concede too much to dehumanization. Being "better off" or "worse off" should not be defined simply in material terms or in terms of one's place in the stratification system of a particular society. A profounder understanding of those terms reaches to their social implications. Being "better off" means being accepted and having the necessary conditions for participation in a caring and creative community. At least, that is the theological perspective. Theology also has much to say about sin, about the brokenness of human life, about the tragic necessity to participate in unjust, evil structures and institutions while seeking to bend them toward something better—if only relatively better. But the doctrine of sin must not be stated in such a way that we lose track of what really is good and what really is evil. Sin is sin precisely because it is a deviation from God's intended good. Recognizing as we must that there is sin in this world and, indeed, that all of us are sinners, it remains the task of theology to help us see more clearly what the good is and to try and serve it as best we can.

Some may object that this picture really does miss the point about the meaning of justice. Many believe intuitively that justice, one way or another, means giving people what they deserve. Something inside us responds very negatively when somebody is denied a reward for which he or she has worked very hard. We are also upset when the reward goes to somebody else who did nothing at all to earn it. We are outraged when it is stolen or taken by deception. An economic incentive system seems nicely devised to ensure that those who earn economic goods are the ones who receive them, and not somebody else. Is there not something appealing about every real-life reenactment of the Horatio Alger myths of rags to riches—with somebody making it to the top through sheer perseverance? George Gilder delights in recounting such stories, and he has good ones to tell of poverty-stricken immigrants, etc., who work long, hard hours in pursuit of a creative idea and who, at last, find success and security. We can call the underlying notion of jus*ice compensatory, for it is based on exactness of compensation: We are to be rewarded for doing good, we are punished for doing evil, and we receive precisely nothing for doing nothing. Locke's view of property, which we have already noted, is a compensatory one. Property belongs to people who create it by mixing their labor with nature. They made it, so it should be and is theirs and not somebody else's.

I do not see how a society could wholly dispense with the compensatory approach to justice since society must have some kind of incentive system. At least every known society has had rewards and punishments to mark off the boundary between approved and disapproved behavior. But to make this the ultimate norm for our understanding of justice is to raise serious theological problems. In the first place, it is to subordinate grace to "works." It is to say that our "doing" is what establishes our claim on society, not our "being." When grace is considered to be prior to works, it is what we are that matters most, not what we do. Viewed in a theological perspective, what we *are* is children of God, each of us valued by God without qualification. When justice is framed accordingly it is understood that our basic rights have been given to us by God, not that we have had to earn them.

John Locke, in fact, had all of this about half-right. In his famous formulation of three inalienable rights of "life, liberty, and the pursuit of property," Locke understood the first two rights to be given in our very nature by God. The third right he also considered to be given, but that right is only the right of opportunity. Perhaps even that would not be entirely a compensatory conception if the opportunity to secure property were universally available on a reasonably equal basis, which it certainly is not. But even at best this remains an altogether individualistic conception. It does not convey at all the sense that God has given us the right to be a part of the family of humanity and that our ability to exercise that right has an economic dimension. We must have some property as a given if our being in community is to have meaning at all. Our theory of justice must be *communitarian* before it is compensatory, and its compensatory elements must be for the sake of the well-being of persons in community.

But there is also another problem with the compensatory view: We never really *know* who earns or deserves everything. The way the world actually works, luck and deception play important roles. Rewards as well as penalties are often grossly disproportionate to accomplishments or failures. Corporate executives sometimes receive huge salaries and bonuses even while their companies are losing money. In 1984 the U.S. auto industry recorded strong profits after several years of struggle, and corporate managers were rewarded with large bonuses. One of the reasons for the profits was a willingness on the part of the labor unions to take pay cuts. Was justice served? Celebrity status in entertainment and athletics can separate actors or athletes of fairly comparable ability, with some receiving exorbitant incomes and others very little. Meanwhile, in the socialist countries, who would care to argue seriously that the most highly rewarded officials are in their positions strictly on the basis of merit? In the case of the Soviet Union, Czechoslovakia, North Korea, and a number of other such countries, one's ability as a survivor and sometimes as a ruthless manipulator may play as important a role in one's compensation as one's ability as a contributor to the social good. So the practical problem of accurately fitting rewards to contributions is not so easy. But even if it were, the deeper question would remain. Before God, do any of us have a right to proclaim our superiority? And if not before God, then before one another? Half the point of St. Paul's emphasis on the priority of grace to works seems to be that none should boast (Rom. 3:27). When a Charles

Murray announces flatly that "some people are better than others" he is treading on very dangerous ground, morally—particularly if he thinks he knows who they are and more particularly if he includes himself among them. Those ultimate judgments are better left to God, who alone knows the secrets of the heart and whose boundless love for all of us both elevates each of us beyond our wildest imaginations and levels our pretensions. More will have to be said later about incentives and about the importance of making an active contribution to the community. But contributing to the community is for its own sake and one's own fulfillment in response to the gifts of life and love; it is not in order to earn or deserve anything.

Taking the Standpoint of the Poor

We can now understand why the liberation theologians are right in saying that Christians should identify with poor people in a special way. It is not that poor people are morally superior to others, or even that they necessarily have greater insight into the causes of their own poverty. It is that they reveal the point of greatest social weakness; they are the weakest link in the social chain. Therefore, they are the point of highest priority. To be poor is to suffer physically or to be estranged socially, or both at once. It is to embody the frustration of God's loving purposes, for God does not intend that there be persons who suffer physically or are estranged socially.

What about the Christian attitude toward the wealthy and prosperous? Are they not also the children of God? A moralistic attitude toward wealth and poverty might exclude them, but that is hardly possible among those who put grace before works. It may not even be realistic, since poverty is not always caused by the actions of rich and prosperous people. Certainly these people are also children of God. But the point is that we deal with their (or our) spiritual need best as we deal with the poor. For the poverty of poor people also represents the estrangement of the rich. They, too, are diminished by the existence of poverty. It is ultimately no privilege to be rich where others are poor; it is a burden, it is a fragmentation of one's own humanity. To cure the disease of poverty is to heal the entire social body. One cannot dwell within that body, either as rich or poor, and not be affected fundamentally by its sickness or health. So taking the standpoint of the poor is also taking the standpoint of the rich, but it is doing so in the only way it can be done.

But how *is* it to be done? How *do* we go about taking the standpoint of the poor?

One obvious answer is to identify with the poor in their revolutionary discontent—even to help arouse that sense of outrage among the poor that will help to fuel revolutionary change. That is an important element in the writings of different kinds of liberation theologians as well as others who employ conflict models of social change. There is something to be said for it. Change toward social justice rarely is initiated from the top. And when it is, it is rarely successful in the absence of a social movement based primarily among poor people themselves. The late Saul Alinsky scored notable successes with methods of social change emphasizing the arousal of deep discontent among poor people, and one way or another that has been characteristic of most successful social revolutions. As long as poor people appear to be content with their lot, it is difficult to mobilize enough social energy to transform systems of privilege—even though, as we have said, it is in the deeper moral interest of the privileged themselves for such transformation to occur.

But there is a problem if the focus is only on arousing discontent among the disinherited. They may be lured into defining life in those same individualistic, competitive terms—only seeking a better outcome for themselves in the competition. Victorious in the struggle to overcome social oppression, they may themselves even become the oppressors of tomorrow. That is the moral risk where the focus of discontent is placed only on one's own plight and not on the fragmented community as a whole. The moral (and practical) genius of the campaigns of Martin Luther King, Jr., and M.K. Gandhi lay in their ability to arouse discontent with oppression while simultaneously evoking love of the oppressor. That reflects moral genius because it more profoundly diagnoses the moral situation, in which no one may justly claim moral superiority but in which an unjust system diminishes the humanity of all. It reflects practical genius because it reduces the element of threat in social change: the well-being of all is clearly intended.

Thus, by taking the standpoint of the poor we are also challenged to develop policies and institutions that relieve all of us of the blight of poverty.

Welfare Reform and Income Security

In a money economy, one obvious point of attack on the problem of poverty is to try to ensure that everybody has enough money. The question of what kinds of social welfare benefits should be provided by government has vexed societies since the beginning of the Industrial Revolution. The English poor laws, the Speenhamland experiment in guaranteed income, the family allowances programs of many Western countries, the various social welfare programs of the Marxist socialist countries, the U.S. Aid to

Families with Dependent Children (AFDC) program, and many others represent efforts to address the needs of people who are economically and socially vulnerable. In the main and on the whole these programs have not been adequate to meet the need as we have defined it here. That is, they have not been sufficient to provide an economic base enabling people to participate normally in the life of the community. In the United States, for instance, a combination of welfare programs has left more than 20 million people below the officially defined poverty line even during the best years (from the mid-1960s to the mid-1970s), and at this writing more than 30 million people live below that level.[8]

One continues to hear it said, however, that welfare benefits are too high and that they should represent a social stigma in order to make them less attractive as a substitute for gainful employment. George Gilder states the point as bluntly as any other widely read author: "There is no such thing as a good method of artificial income maintenance. The crucial goal should be to restrict the system as much as possible, by making it unattractive and even a bit demeaning."[9] Gilder is partly concerned about the public's having to pay for such things. But he also believes that it is more destructive to encourage dependency on the public dole than it is to make the system restrictive and demeaning to its recipients. We have already noted Gilder's belief that "in order to succeed, the poor need most of all the spur of their poverty."

The same point is massively asserted by Charles Murray's book *Losing Ground,* which attempts to document the view that welfare programs developed in the United States during the 1960s and 1970s have served to increase, not decrease, poverty.[10] Murray argues that welfare programs have served as a powerful disincentive to work and that they have undermined, not supported, the families of poor people. Demoralized young people, particularly black young people, have accepted the notion that society is responsible for their plight and that serious educational achievement and work effort are irrelevant to their futures. While over the long run this outlook is disastrous for those who hold it, in the short run the pattern of welfare benefits often makes it more advantageous for young unmarried mothers to remain unmarried and to stay unemployed. Children reared in such circumstances are often demoralized, lacking parental stimulus and support to build different kinds of lives for themselves. Murray's views are supported by an impressive array of data drawn from thirty years of American experience with poverty, social welfare programs, unemployment, and education. His conclusion is that social welfare programs should be drastically reduced and defederalized and that serious educational reforms should be undertaken, including development of a voucher system permitting parents to choose their children's schools and carefully ensuring that children have the opportunity to participate in educational programs for which they are qualified by virtue of admission examinations. Murray specifically advocates the abolition of all affirmative action policies as morally wrong and damaging to the very groups supposed to benefit from them.

As a sweeping critique of liberal economic and social reforms of the past two decades in America, Murray's work has aroused substantial and perhaps needed debate. Many of the programs probably need criticism in light of actual experience with their effects, and a number of his specific proposals (such as those designed to improve actual educational opportunity and achievement) may be well worth considering.[11] But in the context of this chapter, the question he poses is especially fundamental. It is whether it is *possible* to reform social welfare policies and programs in such a way that poverty is greatly diminished if not abolished. For all the massiveness of his supporting data, Murray has been criticized for overlooking information that would not support his conclusions. Phillip Keisling notes, for instance, that Murray has grossly overstated the amount of welfare money that has actually gone to poor people over the past twenty-five years and that he has neglected the fact that states like Mississippi with the lowest AFDC payments should evidence stronger family life and work commitments—which they do not.[12] Keisling also wonders why Murray has failed to see the positive family and employment records of countries with much more generous welfare provisions than the United States. Robert Samuelson points out that Murray neglected the effects of broader economic currents in the 1970s in charging welfare programs with responsibility for increasing poverty during that period.[13] Samuelson also criticizes Murray for minimizing the good done by governmental programs, such as food stamps in virtually eliminating hunger and Medicaid in greatly increasing health care among poor people.

Other criticisms could be added. Murray does not even mention some programs like school lunches, which have improved the nutritional well-being of poor children enormously, helping to lay foundations in health for better mental and social development. Nor, in advocating that welfare programs be defederalized, does he indicate how poor cities and states would be able to manage the load without the assistance of wealthier parts of the country. Would the very wealthy suburbs of Westchester County, New York, feel obligated to assist the South Bronx slums? Would Connecticut feel any accountability for dealing with destitution in Mississippi?

Murray is right in suggesting that particular segments of the poverty population—such as demoralized youth—require very special and highly creative forms of treatment (although his own proposals may not be nearly imaginative enough). But viewing statistics on poverty in general over the past quarter-century in a different way, one is struck by two things: First, the attack on poverty in the 1960s was most successful insofar as it sought to reach those who might reasonably be expected to work. Second, a large majority of the poor after the mid-1960s were either already employed, but at low wages, or were aged, handicapped, single women with family responsibilities, or children—the latter constituting, at 40 to 50 percent, by far the largest segment. Murray's underlying contention that there were many more mothers with illegitimate children as a result of the welfare programs might, to the extent it is really true, argue for some new twists in such programs—although he has surely overlooked other social factors, including the continued reality of racism, in the demoralization of contemporary American inner-city life.

But the question we must address first is whether society is willing to make a serious commitment to undergirding the economic and social needs of its poorest people. The conclusion that the best way to do this is to dismantle welfare programs wholesale simply will not do. To make the only economic life-support systems available to poor people materially inadequate and "a bit demeaning" is to make the practical exclusion of such people from the normal life of the community a matter of deliberate public policy. We will address the problem of work and work opportunity in the next chapter, but here we are faced with the question whether income should necessarily be tied to work. Moralistic social policy will invariably do so; it will insist on a stigma's being attached even when poor people have no realistic opportunity to earn their own income. It will put work before grace at the point where that matters in translating theological doctrine into social practice.

But a social policy that places higher priority on the acceptance of people than it does on what can be gotten out of them will address the need more directly. Various proposals have in fact been worked out over the past generation. Some of these have been advanced by conservative economists like Milton Friedman, who, although he does not advocate very generous levels of support, recognizes that society must meet at least the minimal needs of poor people. The relevant debate among economists and policy-makers who support some form of guaranteed minimum income includes such questions as (1) the level at which the program should be pitched; (2) the percentage of earned income a recipient should be allowed to keep over the basic income grant; (3) the relationship between cash income and economic benefits "in kind" (direct provision of what is needed rather than of cash); (4) the level of government at which benefits should be supplied; (5) the method of policing to avoid fraudulent abuse; (6) the relationship between income guarantees and guaranteed work opportunity.

The technical problems involved in such questions extend beyond the scope of this book, although the basic problems have been worked out depending on the priorities society wishes to pursue.[14] In some respects the key technical question is the second one—the question of how much earned income a welfare-grant recipient should be permitted to keep above the grant itself. That entails important decisions about the relationship between the "working poor" and the unemployed. The basic philosophy of the Negative Income Tax proposal of Milton Friedman and others is to allow welfare recipients to retain some percentage of their earnings from part-time or low-wage employment, accepting frankly the corollary that the "working poor" along with the unemployed will receive some aid. The effect of such a more enlightened policy is to encourage welfare recipients to take such ventures into the job market as they are capable of taking without the fear that their basic income security would thereby be threatened.

The basic strategy should be informed by grace and the desire to incorporate all people into the life of the community; it should not be distorted by crude—and often misguided—moralizing about poor people. Basic security in the conditions of one's existence is necessary if one is to be able to function in society. It may be desirable to maintain some relationship between income and work, but it is theologically sound and practically wise to guarantee security in the former in order to provide a foundation for the latter. If basic security can be counted on by all members of society, increased income and other material benefits may then be developed as added incentives to work.

So far we have addressed this problem largely in terms of the basic income needs of the poorest people in a money economy, for this is the point of greatest human vulnerability. But if the pattern of distribution of wealth and income is to serve the relational needs of the whole community, there is much to be said for making provision for some forms of economic consumption on a communitywide basis—thus guaranteeing secure access to some things regardless of the accidents and intentions of personal wealth-creation. That is already accepted without much question at certain points. Everybody receives police and fire protection, for instance, even though such services are paid for by taxes proportioned roughly to the ability to pay. We all have access to the roads and parks and schools, regardless of our economic circumstances.

Some conservatives (including Friedman) obviously prefer a society in which there is much fine-tuning of the costs of public services so that nobody gets something for nothing and each person pays precisely the cost of each service. But that is a poor model for genuine human community. It is better to exend the family principle as far as possible, with as many facilities and services readily and freely available to all as the economy can sustain. That principle has been extended into the area of education (what a blunder it would be to weaken that!), and some countries have recognized that basic health care should be provided by the community at large. The United States could learn much from Great Britain at that point. Transportation, at least within urban areas, could be more heavily subsidized by the community as a whole. Higher education could also be provided more freely, so that every young person could absolutely count on pursuing advanced studies and training without having to carry great burdens of debt and so that middle- and lower-class parents would not have to spend half their lives anxiously preparing to educate their children. A community in which people could live without worrying about financing the education of their young, or about catastrophic illness, or about insecurity in old age would be a more human place to live, particularly if that community also provided real work opportunity and incentive for all of its members.

The Problem of Inflation

The inflation rate was so severe in several Western countries during the 1970s that many people came to feel that this was the worst possible calamity. We have already noted that the effects of inflation are distributed unevenly, so what is a problem for some people can even be a solution for others. Inflation is generally inequitable in its effects, and it is also unpredictable. While one may benefit from inflation today, one may be destroyed by it tomorrow. Severe inflation can be an important enemy to both economic security and equitable distribution of wealth and income.

The inflation of the 1970s was diagnosed in various ways, ranging from the effects of basic resource scarcity (particularly energy, with the tightening of the international oil cartel) to deficit spending by government, rapid expansion of consumer credit, and the push for higher wages by organized labor. Most of the explanations contain a germ of truth. But the aspect of inflation I wish to emphasize here is the degree to which it reflects the expectations and pressures of organized groups within society. A government may wish to maintain an orderly expansion of the money supply, keeping it within the limits of growing productivity. But since money represents credit relationships that are not completely controllable by government and since the dominant economic groups within society also have considerable political power, prices and wages can easily move beyond those limits. Market forces alone do not provide sufficient restraint—politics and culture are also deeply implicated in the dynamics of economic inflation.

When it is said that a certain rate of unemployment is necessary in order to avoid inflation (as in the typical application of the Phillips Curve which we have already mentioned), the point is not that there is a necessary mathematical relationship of cause and effect involved. Rather, it is that workers will not be sufficiently restrained in their wage demands unless there is some fear of unemployment on their part. They must have a sufficiently large number of unemployed people to compete against. If workers showed restraint in their wage demands, full employment would not necessarily be inflationary. There have been noninflationary periods of near-full employment historically (such as the early 1960s in the U.S.) and, for that matter, the percentage of unemployment deemed necessary to restrain inflation has been creeping up in recent years—so we are dealing here with culturally relative expectations as much as with natural forces. The success of the Reagan administration in the U.S. in curbing inflation in the early 1980s was partly due to the partial collapse of the OPEC cartel and the resultant stabilization of petroleum prices. But it was also due, perhaps in larger measure, to the administration's (and the Federal Reserve Board's) tight monetary and fiscal policies leading to business failures and unemployment. Expectations were sharply curbed, and decisions were increasingly made on a noninflationary basis. Whether one approves of what happened depends largely on whether one regards the disease or the cure as having been worse, for the country paid a fearful price in the highest rate of unemployment since the Great Depression in order to bring inflation under control. And it is also questionable, in the long run, whether the burden of stopping the inflation was borne equitably within society. Administration policies led to the first substantial increases in many years in wealth of the upper 20th percentile of the population relative to the rest, and the unemployed themselves (of course) bore the major brunt of the policies. But inflation was sharply curtailed, and the reelection of Ronald Reagan to the presidency in 1984 probably reflected public gratitude for that as much as anything else.

Earlier, Democratic Party administrations in the 1960s had applied preventive medicine with equal success, although perhaps more equitably. The famous "jawboning" techniques of Presidents Kennedy and Johnson induced management and labor in key industries to abate their demands. Bringing as much political and economic pressure to bear as those administrations could, both management and labor were forced to lower their

expectations below what they could have gotten through pure exploitation
of market economics. (President Nixon, whose economic principles
would not allow him to continue even this mild form of political intervention in the economic sphere, soon found it necessary to undertake the
much more severe medicine of out-and-out wage and price controls as he
sought to prepare the economic climate of the country suitably for his
reelection in 1972.)

The point to gain from all this is twofold: First, inflation must be
evaluated in terms of its relationship to other economic forces and relationships and not by itself alone. And second, inflation reflects the expectations and pressures of social groups—it is not simply a result of imper-
sonal market forces.

Fairness in Wages and Prices

Were there any generally agreed-on standards of fairness by which
prices and wages could be set, this would perhaps not be a problem.
Increases and decreases in prices and wages could be managed uniformly
and equitably in order to avoid the twin demons of inflation and recession.
Full employment would pose no problems. It would be an unmixed bless-
ing. But there are no such agreed-on standards. Those who are highest on
the scale of wealth and income usually regard their privileged position as
a matter of right, and they tend to view any closing of the gap between
themselves and the less privileged as an injustice in the light of their own
superior contributions to society. If anything, they believe their own status
should be improved. (A *Washington Post* survey in the late 1970s discovered, in fact, that many people in the upper income brackets tended to
measure themselves by those who were still higher above them, not by the
vast majority who were lower on the socioeconomic scale. Hence even
these very prosperous people remained somewhat dissatisfied with their
lot.) People who are lower in income and wealth tend to think of justice as
"catching up." Thus, pure equality is regarded as justice by some and
injustice by others.

In light of this and the intricate complexity of the system of wages and
prices in any modern economy, it is no wonder that economists and policy-makers tend to prefer a simple market determination of wages and
prices so that businesspersons and workers are left free to get whatever
they can for their products and services on the open market. But that, as
we have seen, is not very satisfactory either. For an absolutely free and
open market will result in either inflation or recession or both.

The concept of fairness in wages and prices has yet another reference
point, at least in the minds of consumers and workers: precedence. People

tend to measure what is fair on the basis of what has been accepted as generally fair for a long period of time, with allowance for small changes. This is why it is difficult for businesspeople to make abrupt, large-scale increases in prices without disrupting markets and losing business in the process—even if the law of supply and demand would seem to indicate that such increases could be made. When a given market has grown accustomed to a particular range of prices, major changes have to be introduced artfully. This is also why it is difficult to introduce major changes in the relationships of compensation provided for different jobs. Those who catch up or move ahead as a result of such changes will accept them all right; but others will regard them as unfair. Prior to the unionization of garbage collectors in many cities, such workers were very poorly paid. The unfairness of their wages seemed clear enough, particularly in light of the hard physical labor and unpleasant surroundings involved. But dramatic increases in their wages (particularly in cities like San Francisco) were first criticized by people who saw the gap closing between the pay of lowly garbage collectors and their own pay, and they were threatened by it.

If anything, these few pages may have understated the complexity of the problem. But this is a dilemma that is not likely to go away. Every alternative seems unacceptable. The reliance on pure market forces is potentially disruptive of society. Centralized planning has no agreed set of standards on which it could set "fair" prices and wages, and even if it did have such standards it might lose important values by setting the market principle aside entirely. And accustomed relationships among prices and wages, important as they are in determining the behavior of consumers and workers, are often indefensible on ethical grounds.

The dilemma is not a new one. Medieval thought on justice in wages and prices offers comparatively little help today, based as it was on obsolete conceptions of money and hostile as it seemed to postfeudal economic development. But the concepts of just price and just wage at least stand as a reminder that economic equity is a serious question for ethical inquiry and community decision-making. Pope Leo XIII's conception of the just wage is suggestive. Leo regarded the just wage as the sum required to sustain the worker and his family. In some respects this is a naïve doctrine, since it does not face up to the problem of how an employer could pay different workers different wages for the same kind of work, based on variable family sizes and needs, and still meet the disciplines of competition in the free market. Nevertheless, Leo's doctrine is a reminder that human need should ultimately be the determining factor in income.

The general standard stated above can be affirmed: that all members of society should have available to them the material conditions necessary to their functioning as members of the community. But how can that general criterion be translated into actual wage and price policy? I cannot offer any easy answers, but several observations may be in order.

First, it is probably a mistake to discard any of the three approaches to wage- and price-setting mentioned above: the market, centralized planning, and continuity with previous custom. But since only centralized planning entails the community's assumption of full responsibility for its own destiny, special attention needs to be given to its possibilities and limitations. Centralized planning does well to respect broad areas of freedom in economic life, making limited but real use of the market principle. The wisdom of that is certainly underscored by the floundering of a number of the socialist economies when they have been too rigid in their economic planning. People need space for creativity without having to check every move with central authority, and there is some truth in the view that the market can allocate goods and services rationally in accordance with the actual wishes of buyers and sellers. At the same time, the community does well to respect some continuity in the customary structure of prices and relationships—at least up to a point. Abrupt changes are sometimes needed to correct blatant injustices (as in the case of the American sharecroppers, migrant workers, and garbage collectors); but other changes can be made more gradually.

Second, governmental income and price policy can set broad parameters within which wages and prices can fluctuate. The principle of minimum wages has been established in the United States, the United Kingdom, and other countries. While still bitterly opposed by advocates of absolute laissez-faire, the principle has generally proved to be a good one. It helps protect the humanity of workers and emphasize the doctrine that labor is not just another commodity. It has the effect of announcing to employers that if their enterprises cannot be productive with a work force compensated at least at minimum wage levels, then the community is better off without such enterprises. There has been much less attention paid to the question whether incomes should be limited at the upper end. The graduated–income tax principle, currently under serious attack in the United States, does acknowledge that some redistribution of income is the proper business of government. But even that has proved vulnerable to tax loopholes and the expatriation of wealth. In a society where it is increasingly difficult to identify differences of contribution to the total economic effort, there is something to be said for limiting the gap between the richest and poorest members of the community. In the arts and athletics, the differences between marginal and exorbitant incomes are often little more than the accidents of celebrity status. The difference between the best athletes and artists and the highly competent second echelon is hardly enough to justify the vast differences in compensation. The difference between highly paid doctors and the comparatively poorly compensated nurses and paramedics, in terms of training and competence, may be enough to warrant some differential in income—but hardly to the extent typical of the United States. It may be time for serious attention to be given to measures placing some limits on the upper reaches of income. That could have the effect of spreading total economic resources more widely and fairly; it could also improve social relationships.

Third, where policies of government cannot directly determine wages and prices without too great a distortion of market forces, government can itself redistribute wealth more equitably. We have already discussed the problem of welfare reform and proposed, along with others, that more serious attention be given to a program of public aid not only for the unemployed but also for the working poor. Currently a certain stigma attaches to public assistance programs (though not, curiously, to public subsidization of the affluent!). The assumption behind the stigma is utterly unrealistic—namely, that it is possible and desirable for every person to be totally self-reliant. That assumption flies in the face of the deeper reality of our being-in-community; it is questionable in light of the most basic religious and philosophical traditions of Western civilization. Persons need to be encouraged to be self-reliant, all right, but in a communal context. To be in community is to share in its burdens and responsibilities, to make one's contributions to the welfare of others, but also to receive the contributions of others with gratitude and without shame. When the community places a floor underneath the economic status of every person through appropriate social welfare programs it is enhancing the life of all. It is in everybody's interest that there not be poor people. That is obviously true in the case of children (and nearly 40 percent of the poor people of America are children under the age of 18), for the effects of poverty seriously diminish the ability of poor children to become fully contributing members of the community later on. But it is also true in the case of adults, for their poverty contributes to all kinds of social pathology and, in subtler ways, undermines the moral self-esteem of the more affluent.

Would a national commitment to eradicate poverty through bold strokes of income redistribution seriously undermine economic productivity in contemporary societies? It might to some extent if there remained no relationship between work and income, but nobody is seriously proposing that. The most responsible proposals for welfare reform are based on the negative–income tax principle, which preserves some economic incentive—as we have just seen. But the other side of the coin is that serious attention be paid to employment and educational policies, which we will do in the next chapter.

Tax Reform

The system of taxation is one of the most powerful instruments available to society in accomplishing social goals. The goal of encouraging contributions to charitable institutions is furthered in the United States by allowing taxpayers to deduct the amount of their contributions from their income for the purpose of computing their income-tax liability. Similarly, the goal of encouraging homeownership in the U.S. has been furthered substantially by allowing homeowning taxpayers to deduct mortgage interest and property-tax payments. A host of other similar deductions and exemptions are written into the U.S. Tax Code in order to achieve this or that social purpose, some intended, some not.

Discussions of economic equity cannot be concluded without noting that any nation's tax structure will profoundly affect the proportionate shares of income and wealth of its people. Since 1913 when the U.S. adopted the graduated–income tax principle by constitutional amendment, the federal income tax has bulked larger and larger as an instrument of national economic policy. It is based on the assumption that taxes on income are, overall, the fairest reflections of ability to pay and that people should be taxed at higher rates as their income rises. The latter assumption implicitly means that the income-tax system should be used to redistribute economic resources from more affluent to less affluent people. The extent to which it really does so is debatable. The pattern of tax deductions, exemptions, and exclusions available to wealthier people, combined with the lowering of tax rates in the higher brackets, has had the effect of diminishing the tax share of the affluent and thrusting more of the burden back on those of lesser means. That is particularly evident when one factors in the many state and local sales taxes, which tend to thrust more of the burden on those who must use a higher proportion of their income in consumption, and the lowering of corporate, estate, gift, and capital-gains tax rates in recent years. The Economic Recovery Tax Act of 1981, one of the centerpieces of the then-new Reagan Administration, substantially decreased the redistributive effects of the tax system. Ronald Pasquariello, a Christian ethicist and student of the technicalities of tax reform, has concluded that the tax system as a whole is no longer progressive or redistributive in its overall effects:

> The point is that in 1966, the system was at best proportional—the same percentage was extracted from everyone's income. Since that time, as shown

above, the progressive taxes have been cut back for a variety of reasons and the regressive taxes have increased sharply. The compelling conclusion is that the tax system is regressive. Since it is the middle class who have experienced the largest distortion in their taxes, it is the middle class who bears the burden of the tax system.[15]

The technicalities of tax reform lie beyond the scope of this volume, but two things should be observed: First, that inequalities of wealth and income in the prosperous countries of Europe and North America make substantial redistribution a moral imperative. Second, that in the effort to use the tax system to accomplish this purpose one must be wary of assuming that any particular reform will necessarily have that effect without examining it closely. No particular form of tax is necessarily progressive or regressive apart from the way it is structured. Sales taxes are usually regressive, placing a heavier burden on the poor; but a sales tax limited to luxury items consumed only by the wealthy would be progressive. Abolition of most current income-tax deductions might be progressive, but deductions can be structured in a quite progressive way. A Value Added Tax, such as those widely utilized in Europe currently, can be either regressive or progressive depending on what exactly is taxed and at what rates.

One must view the prospect of sweeping tax reform with either alarm or eager anticipation, depending on one's ethical assessment of the current tax system of one's own country and on one's appraisal of the political forces arrayed for or against one's hoped-for reforms.

CHAPTER SEVEN

Priority Three: Employment and Educational Opportunity

> *. . . to the objection that work and self-respect are inseparable, the major reply is that the real necessity is not for a production job, but for meaningful activity. This may or may not be related to income.*
>
> —Michael D. Reagan (1964)[1]

Work is an important aspect of human fulfillment, as Michael Reagan (not at all to be confused with his more famous namesake) has noted. But as we also observed in chapter 3, work needs to be defined more broadly than it usually is. When most peole think of "work" they think of a job that one gets paid for doing. But if work is a moral and theological category, and not simply an economic one, then it must be understood more broadly. It is indeed "work" to be employed on an automobile assembly line or as a salesperson in a department store or as a public schoolteacher. But it is also "work" to paint one's own living room on one's day off or to teach a church-school class on Sunday morning or to cook dinner. Both the college teacher and the college student are "working," although the former is paid for the effort expended while the latter must pay for the privilege. The economy—any economy in the modern world—would break down without the efforts of people to earn a livelihood. But any society would also disintegrate if it were deprived of the contributions people make without financial compensation. So the term "work" must have a broader meaning than we usually associate with employment.

Of course, the vocational understanding of work is also narrower, as we also noted before. A moral understanding of work connects it with purposes that contribute in some way to the betterment of the human situation. Much gainful employment can be vocational in that sense; some cannot. Much purely voluntary work can also be vocational while, again, some cannot. Most people are involved in both compensated and uncompensated forms of work. And we may venture to say that most people are also doing some things that contribute positively to human life and some things that do not.

The Importance of Opportunity to Work

In any case, work is very important to human fulfillment. That is obviously true in countries like the United States and Switzerland and Great Britain which have been influenced greatly by the "work ethic" cultural tradition. In such countries considerable stigma is attached to idleness, and the self-esteem of most people is involved in whether they perceive themselves to be contributing members of the community. But something more than the cultural peculiarities of some Western countries is involved here. It is also a question of basic human nature. Can we be fully human if we are mainly passive in our orientation on life? Is it enough just to exist? The biblical response to that is a resounding no. Its portrait of human life emphasizes action in service to God. While the many references to faith and trust (including St. Paul's famous contrast between faith and works) might convey the impression to some that faith means only the acceptance of whatever happens, it is clear in context that faith and trust are active, not passive, virtues. To be in faith is to be faithful. It is to *respond* to what we believe God has done for us. And if we do not respond, actively and joyfully, the gift of God's love cannot be actualized in our living experience. So James writes that "faith by itself, if it has no works, is dead" (James 2:17). Work, seen in this perspective, is not what we do to earn God's grace or love, for that has already been given freely. The fact that we know ourselves to be loved makes it possible for us to work without a sense of compulsion. Freed of compulsion, our work is genuinely creative. It is doing good for the sake of the good that is to be done, whether or not that is also what we happen to be paid for under a specific economic arrangement. When we do good for the sake of the good our lives find new levels of fulfillment. Seen in theological perspective, this means that we are contributing to the achievement of God's own purposes. There is real meaning in what we do, for the good that we do will endure. Seen in a psychological perspective, work seems necessary to bring life into integrated focus. When our energies are directed toward goals, a unified and growing selfhood develops. Passivity, on the other hand, leads to disintegration of the self.

Work also seems important to our social fulfillment. Human relationship cannot be purely passive. Relationship involves receiving as well as giving, but it also involves giving as well as receiving. Our work is contribution to others, not just for ourselves. I doubt that many people could long sustain creative work if it had to be conducted entirely in isolation from others, but I also doubt that many could be in community without making their contribution to its life. Farmers relate to more than sun and rain and soil and the nurturing of plants from sowing to harvest; they also relate to those whom their work is destined to feed. Mechanics relate to more than automobiles; they also serve those who need transportation. Merchants relate to more than inventories and cash registers; they also help provide necessities to those who come to buy. Artists engage in more than art for art's sake; they also deepen the sensitivities of those who will listen and see. And I suspect that even the most reclusive of artists do their work for some kind of audience, imagined or real. Not all work really does benefit our fellow human beings; some is even harmful. But the work we do for one another is still the bloodstream without which human relationship would break apart altogether. To be able to interact meaningfully with others means that we must contribute as well as receive the contributions of others.

To be deprived of the opportunity to work is therefore something worse than the simple loss of income, bad as that usually is. For without meaningful work opportunity, we are dehumanized. We lose a sense of self and we lose an important linkage with others in the life of society. An early draft of the Catholic bishops' pastoral on the U.S. economy puts this poignantly:

> The unemployed come often to feel that they are worthless, without a productive role in society, in part because of the pervasive tendency in our society to blame the unemployed for unemployment, an assessment they often internalize. Each day and in scores of ways our society tells them, We don't need your talent, we don't need your initiative, we don't need you. Historical research indicates that very few people survive long periods of unemployment without some psychological damage even if they have enough funds to meet their needs.[2]

We should not be surprised to learn that social pathologies of various kinds often accompany unemployment. In his studies of this phenomenon, Harvey Brenner discovered that each percentage-point increase in the rate of unemployment correlates with a 4.3 percent increase in first-time admissions to mental hospitals, a 4.1 percent increase in the suicide rate, a 4 percent rise in the prison population, and a 5.7 percent increase in homicides. Each 1 percent increase in unemployment in the United States is also, he found, accompanied by about 37,000 deaths related to stress—such as heart attacks.[3] Commenting on unemployment in Great Britain, Social Democratic Party leader David Owen expresses particular alarm about the effect of unemployment on the young:

Young people who on leaving school or after higher education search in vain for a job for months, which can stretch into years, are likely to feel—and with some justice—that they have been rejected by society. That some of them should take refuge in alcohol or drugs or crime is hardly surprising; but it is a searing indictment of the failure by the societies in which they have grown up to provide them with a fundamental human right: the right to work. . . . It does not seem particularly fanciful to discern, in high rates of long-term unemployment among the young, the seeds of a threat to our democratic system.[4]

Unemployment is, in fact, a worldwide phenomenon of alarming proportions. It has affected Western Europe and North America's highly developed economies with the pathological effects noted above. The effects may be even more profound in Third World settings, where economic development cannot begin to keep pace with population growth and displacement of people from traditional work on the land. Urban settings everywhere, but particularly in the Third World, witness the disintegration of persons and of civilized community life that occurs when large numbers of people are unable to play a role in the life of the city.

Private- and Public-Sector Employment

Cheap answers to the problem of unemployment are readily available. Perhaps the cruelest of all is the view that people who really want to work will always be able to find a job or make one for themselves. George Gilder delights in recounting stories of diligent immigrants starting from scratch with small "mom and pop" enterprises and from this base rising to entrepreneurial heights—thus echoing the Horatio Alger themes of the early part of this century. No doubt there are many such life histories. But this kind of economic success may be more elusive than the Gilders and Algers suppose, even at the entry level. Bearing in mind that unemployment statistics in the United States record only the numbers of people who have actively sought work, it is clear that their failure is not simply in a lack of desire for work! It is, rather, in their inability to get hired. What this comes down to is that when (as at this moment of writing) the unemployment rate is recorded as 7.3 percent, it means that more than 8 million Americans seeking work have been unable to find it. No doubt many of these are people who are unqualified for available work. No doubt some may be faulted for not doing what they could do to qualify themselves. No doubt quite a few of these unemployed have not exhibited traits of imaginative enterprise on the basis of which they could launch successful businesses of their own—bearing in mind, of course, that there has been an increase in small-business failures in recent years even among those who did make a venture in that direction. But what really cannot be doubted is the great unevenness of opportunity.

When conservative thinkers proclaim as their great objective that this should be an "opportunity society," they seldom emphasize the concrete conditions of human well-being and education without which opportunity is reduced to an abstraction. By opportunity they generally mean freedom from business restraint. They mean a market that is structured in such a way that any are free to buy or sell, with as little governmental involvement through regulation and taxation as possible. But what does that kind of opportunity mean to unemployed black youths from the ghetto? Some, in Horatio Alger fashion, will indeed be able to escape the trap, swimming against the stream. Most will not. The tragedy of their lack of initial opportunity is compounded through loss of self-esteem, deepening patterns of life that are not conducive to the disciplines of employment, and hopelessness. The U.S. and Britain and other nations with high levels of youth unemployment are risking the development of a generation of adults who never find rootage in the productive life of society. This may be the worst aspect of the tragedy of unemployment in contemporary industrial civilization.

But even those who have long years of experience in the work force confront society with another poorly understood tragedy. It is all very well to say to unemployed steel or auto workers that they have every opportunity to seek retraining and to relocate themselves and their families to other parts of the country where work may more readily be available. Many have tried, some successfully. But it is no casual thing to uproot one's family, leaving the settled humanizing relationships of a community where one has lived for many years (and where one's parents and grandparents may also have lived) in quest of what has often proved to be only a chimera of opportunity.

It is therefore thoughtless and unfeeling to blame the unemployed for their plight. Even President Reagan sometimes characterized unemployment in terms that seemed to blame the unemployed. In one speech, Mr. Reagan commented: "Pick up the Sunday paper and look at the number of help-wanted ads. Here are employers begging for employees, taking ads out for them at a time of the highest unemployment that we've known since the war" (December 18,1982). Presumably the unemployed, had they any gumption at all, needed only to pick up the Sunday paper to find themselves a job. Such sentiments hardly do justice to the well-publicized instances of long lines forming in metropolitan centers when employers announced the opening of a few jobs. In another speech the president did acknowledge that the concrete availability of any job depends on whether the applicant is qualified: "In the great metropolitan centers . . . you count as many as 65 pages of help-wanted ads. . . . These newspaper ads convinced us that there are jobs waiting and people not trained for those jobs" (October 4, 1982). But is society to wash its hands of this situation by saying, in effect, that the unemployed can go get themselves trained if they want a job badly enough?

Sar Levitan and Clifford Johnson, who cite these and other interesting quotations from conservative leaders, note with considerable insight that even the structuring of the "safety net" for the "truly needy" is predicated on the assumption that jobs are sufficiently available to the able-bodied.[5] Again, even President Reagan has characterized the "truly needy" in terms that suggest many people have been getting undeserved assistance. "All the cuts we have made in such programs are aimed at taking people off those programs that really are not morally justified in being there" (January 21,1983). A presidential advisor, Martin Anderson, makes the point even more graphically: "If a person is capable of taking care of himself, he is independent and should not qualify for any amount of welfare."[6] But, as Levitan and Johnson point out, everything depends on the job market, on the actual availability of jobs:

> Conservatives have succeeded in challenging the willingness of the poor to work largely by treating job availability as a given. Recognizing that poverty and work motivation can be plausibly linked only if jobs are available for those who seek them, they profess confidence in market mechanisms while ignoring the evident lack of employment opportunities for millions of Americans, not only in recessions but also in good times.[7]

The argument that unemployment chiefly results from the indolence of the unemployed is, in effect, an argument that nothing in particular needs to be, or even can be, done to deal with the problem of employment. Unemployment will straighten itself out if the able-bodied poor come to realize that they cannot rely on government charity to bail them out. That view is absolutely central to the case made by Gilder, Murray, and others for demolishing the whole social welfare system. Confronting the reality of their situation, without the sugarcoating afforded by welfare dependency, the poor may at last be motivated to do something about their own condition. Some social critics who are not quite that judgmental about the poor still feel that employment is primarily, almost exclusively, a private-sector responsibility. Public-sector jobs, evoking memories in the U.S. of the WPA and CCC of the early New Deal, are understood by such people to be dead-end employment. Those who lock themselves into such work receive marginal pay for virtually meaningless work. They find themselves patronized by a public bureaucracy, in a situation with no opportunities for real advancement or career development. Government can help at the margins, for instance by subsidizing private-sector job creation in inner-

city locations or by tax policies that give added incentive to private enterprise in selected areas of high unemployment. Public employment is thus
psychologically and economically suspect, while employment in the private sector alone addresses the real need of people for jobs with a meaningful future in which significant contributions to society can be made.

But is that necessarily so? Are there not forms of public service that
constitute splendid opportunities for people to make important contributions to public good, many of them leading to fulfilling lifelong careers? I
am thinking of schoolteachers, public health workers, agricultural exten-
sion agents, forest rangers, park personnel, firefighters, police, social
workers, nurses in publicly owned and operated hospitals, sanitation
workers, and many others. Even with some decreases in employment in
the U.S. in 1982, nearly 16 million persons were employed by government
at federal, state, and local levels. While this represented only about 14
percent of the total number of employed persons, one could hardly declare
that 14 percent to be unworthy and the remaining 86 percent alone to be
what work really ought to be. Corresponding figures for many of the other
industrial democracies are weighted more heavily toward public employment, although the private sector still dominates in most cases. In part this
reflects the fact that a number of other industrial democracies, such as
Britain, France, and West Germany, have more economic activity organized in the public sector. I would not be prepared to argue that work in
the private sector is necessarily unworthy or meaningless either, of course
(although it must be remembered that millions of the newly created jobs in
the 1970s and 1980s in the private sector have been low-level forms of
employment with little career-development opportunity and sometimes
with no great social significance).

Let us face the truth that some people oppose all public-service employment for ideological reasons. They are so committed to the free-market
mechanism as the solution to all economic problems that they are unable
to absorb even the obvious fact that much public-service employment is
necessary, creative, and fulfilling and that many people are dedicated to
doing that work and doing it well.

At stake in this question of private and public forms of employment is
the question whether society can address the problem of joblessness *directly*. Given high unemployment figures—currently over 7 percent in the
U.S. and much higher in some European and Third World countries—is
there any reason why society should not use the mechanisms of government to create job opportunities for those among the unemployed who
want them? Why should government not become the "employer of last
resort," so that all will be guaranteed job opportunity?

The well-known arguments about government's economic inefficiency stand against this. The claim is that private-sector employment is more efficient in principle because it is situated in a competitive context. Employees might presumably get used to public jobs that would then be perpetuated more or less indefinitely, thereby using resources that would be used more efficiently by private enterprise—again, since private enterprise is subject to the disciplines of market competition and government is not. More and more people might become involved in public employment, probably doing less and less. So a vicious circle would develop, with more and more resources being absorbed into the public sector and fewer and fewer resources available to the private sector where real wealth can be generated.

It is a curious thing that those who denigrate public employment in this way overlook the more obvious points. It is unemployment that absorbs more and more resources, creating vicious circles that are economically and socially costly long into the future. What could be more expensive to society than a wasted generation of inner-city youth? How can we afford to forget the costly pathologies resulting, as we have noted, from each percentage point of increase in unemployment? Are prisons and mental institutuions more efficient users of economic wealth than programs in which the beneficiaries are themselves employed in making some contribution to society? These costs, sometimes hidden from view, are in addition to the more obvious costs of unemployment benefits and welfare payments, the direct-transfer payments a compassionate society provides for those in need.

In sheer economic terms, a distinction can probably be made between the forms of employment government provides by its fiscal policies, that is, by the purchases it makes in the private sector, and job creation in the public sector. During a period of serious budgetary deficits, such as that experienced by the United States in the 1980s, increased public expenditures of the first kind may indeed be too costly. (This is a point that needs to be kept carefully in mind in relation to exorbitant military expenditures, where the cost to the government of each job created in defense industries is unusually high.) But direct job creation for socially worthwhile ends can be productive for two reasons: first, because the capital investment required for such job creation can be relatively moderate (such jobs can be more "labor-intensive" than most industrial employment); second, because such jobs save society the other direct and indirect expenditures. But even if direct provision of jobs in this way did not "make sense" economically, could one argue that it is not a *moral* imperative?

Most people will acknowledge that everybody who wants to work should be able to do so. Some economists still believe that full employment is necessarily inflationary, since full employment provides workers with a sellers' market in which they can continue to increase their wages beyond increases in productivity. That is not necessarily so, as several periods of near-full employment and minimal inflation illustrate. But even if it were true that full employment is inflationary, we must ask whether the unemployed should be forced to bear the cost of a low rate of inflation. Inflation is not necessarily the worst thing for those who otherwise have no work and little income.

It is also argued that if we will be patient a sufficiently stimulated economy will generate all the jobs we need in the private sector. Economic recovery in the 1980s appears more real in the United States than elsewhere. Nineteen eighty-three and 1984 were, in terms of economic growth and job creation, unusually good years, and 1985 evidenced only modest easing of the rate of growth. Unemployment dropped from a high of 10.8 percent in December 1982 to 7.3 percent in 1985 with the prospect of further lowering of the rate in subsequent months and years.[8] It is conceivable that unemployment will drop to what are essentially full-employment rates by the time this book is published, or soon thereafter. But there is a real likelihood that that will not occur or that if it does unemployment will rise again in further turns of the trade cycle. Some economists are less sanguine than others about the vulnerability of the U.S. economy, particularly in light of the dependency of that economy on foreign investment and the fluctuations in world economic and political conditions. The moral problem is that most of the risk must be borne by the presently or potentially unemployed. The fact that unemployment could be as high as 7.3 percent two years after the beginning of a substantial economic recovery at least means that full employment is not a prompt accompaniment to economic growth and prosperity.

In light of this, should not the right to a job for all who want one be a high priority, with direct implementation of that right undertaken by creative governmental programs? I say "creative" governmental programs because it is certainly the case that some kinds of governmental job-creation programs have been anything but that. No doubt the anecdotes of WPA or CCC workers digging ditches and then filling them in are grossly exaggerated. But there may be enough truth to that kind of tale to make us take seriously the task of protecting the "employment of last resort" programs from abuse and mismanagement. Since the priority of a real right to work for all is a high one, it is worth our while to manage it well.

Criteria for Public-Service Employment

"Employment of last resort" programs do well to observe each of the following conditions.

First, the work to be accomplished should be genuinely useful to society, so that those who do it can take pride in what they are doing and be serious about doing it and so that the rest of us will be less tempted to stigmatize the work and the people who do it.

Second, the work should generally be something that would not otherwise be done, so that this will not compete directly with other programs and private enterprise. Presently underfunded conservation programs and programs bringing renewal to inner-city areas come to mind as meeting this and the first criterion. One of the flaws in the unfortunately discontinued U.S. CETA program, which provided training and jobs for youth, was the lack of imagination in the development of program objectives and the lack of discipline in implementation. But such flaws can be corrected.

Third, compensation for the work should be at or slightly above the minimum-wage rate, with some provision for advancement for those who move toward long-term careers in government service. There is no problem with public-service jobs competing with most minimum-wage employment in the private sector, since much of the latter is of modest social significance. But programs of this kind should not be able to compete for workers with most private forms of employment.

Fourth, job discipline should be seriously maintained. Those who do this work should be expected to perform honestly and to acquire disciplined work habits if they do not already have them. For young people presently lacking such work habits, the disciplines of such programs can be extremely important in preparing them for more significant forms of employment in the private or public sectors. Presently, military service often helps young people in this way; ideally public-employment programs should be able to do the same. But for them to do so, serious attention must be given to the patterns and disciplines of work in the real world. U.S. policy-makers might learn something from experiments in London, where such young people are given very concentrated attention by social workers for a period of two years. The sustained direct personal attention has apparently been very helpful in changing attitudes toward work and raising the self-esteem of those who discover, sometimes to their surprise, that they are capable of accomplishing things.

Fifth, employment as a last resort should not be a substitute for or a requirement for welfare payments. But if some form of the negative income tax should be adopted whereby recipients would be permitted to retain a specified percentage of their earned income on top of the basic public grant, the relationship between welfare payments and work income would prove to be the same here as elsewhere in the economy.

Sixth, the work developed should be as interesting as possible, it being understood that all important and challenging work involves aspects of routine and drudgery.

The organization of public-service employment for young people might very well be different than for mature adults. Young people may need more structure. The realities of youth unemployment and the positive effect of a period of military service on many young people have led some people to propose a one- or two-year period of compulsory public service (not necessarily military) for all youth. There is something to be said for this. Such a program, if universal, would not carry social stigma. It could, if well organized, be a valuable experience in the pluralism of contemporary life to those whose lives have been too insulated. It could afford valuable lessons in citizenship and mutual responsibility. For many it could be a helpful transition period from school years to the work force or higher education, especially if it were to incorporate educational aspects. Its universality could make it more efficient than small-scale hit-or-miss programs. Highly motivated young people who are deeply committed to careers in fields requiring many years of preparation (such as medicine or the arts) for whom such delay of one or two years would constitute real hardship might possibly be exempted. Moreover, conscientious objection to particular activities (such as military service) should be honored, with provision for a range of alternatives.

There may be better ways of meeting the need without launching such a universal and compulsory program. But the present plight of the unemployed is unconscionable, particularly in its effects on young people who are just starting out in life. Every year of continued public complacency about this condition adds to the waste and deepens the hopelessness of many of those on whom the future of society depends.

Educational Opportunity and Cultural Development

The provision of educational opportunity for all is a related and very important priority. American society has, at this point, been remarkably successful, in spite of the legitimate complaints about the deteriorating quality of many schools. The U.S. pioneered the concept of universal, free, and compulsory school attendance and has implemented it on a truly massive scale. More than 40 million children and young people were enrolled in public schools in 1982, with an additional 8.4 million in public colleges and universities.[9] Six million exercised their option to attend private schools, with an additional 2.6 million in private colleges and universities. This is a stupendous accomplishment. Quite apart from the intrinsic values of education for its own sake—which are considerable—the principle of universal free education and the ready availability of higher education have had an enormous and positive impact on the economic life of the nation.

The educational developments of the past need to be improved on, but there is some danger that they may instead be diminished. Led by Milton Friedman, many economic conservatives currently advocate the substitution of a voucher system of payment for education for the present direct funding of public schools.[10] Parents would be provided with educational vouchers by the government for each of their children. They would use these vouchers to pay for education at the schools of their choice. Presumably this would make the schools more efficient and creative since they would then have to compete for students against other schools or risk going out of business. The market principle would thus be applied directly to educational institutions. Those who advocate this solution point to the supposed superiority of private schools in general and to the managerial inefficiencies and presumed low morale of teachers in public schools in general. People who advocate the voucher system are not reluctant to offer sweeping generalizations about the superiority of private over public institutions and about the degree of deterioration of the public ones.

Actual adoption of such a voucher system could be a monumental mistake. It could lead to precipitous erosion of many schools without their being replaced outright with better ones. It could lead the better schools to be selective in their enrollment policies, thus screening out pupils with more marginal backgrounds, thus reinforcing and deepening a class pattern in social life. In some areas it could reinforce subtle forms of racism. A true conservative, faced with such massive change in the educational institutions of the land, might well ask why we should tamper so drastically with what has, in world-historical terms, been such a successful set of institutions. Changes of lesser scale may indeed be needed—such as modification of tenure provisions for teachers so that a teacher would have to demonstrate his or her effectiveness for a longer period of years before gaining the security of life-long appointment. And in general the public has a right to hold teachers and administrators to high standards of competence.

But it may be that improvements in educational quality really require increases in public funding. Compensation of teachers generally lags behind that of comparably trained professionals in other areas, and the ratio of students to teachers is often not conducive to much personal interaction between them. Sometimes the most poorly funded schools are precisely the ones in the inner-city areas where a higher concentration of teaching talent and compensatory opportunity is needed. Some of the problems of

low self-esteem and lack of self-discipline that affect later employment
opportunity need to be addressed much more vigorously in the schools.
Charles Murray does well to emphasize the educational problems of youth
in large and troubled urban schools, but it is astonishing that he neglects
what is obviously an important part of the answer: to make such education
much more personal by greatly increasing the number of teachers or other
adult educational aides.[11] Possibly conservatives like him are unduly inhib-
ited by the fact that this would substantially increase the cost of education!
But the proposed voucher system strikes me as a frivolous answer to a
serious range of problems.

The principle of free education is well established in this and other
industrialized countries up through age 16 or 18. The principle is not as
clear at the level of higher education. The most massive breakthrough in
making higher education available to all occurred almost inadvertently in
the United States following World War II when millions of veterans were
given GI Bill educational benefits. College and university enrollments expanded dramatically. In recent years educational grants and loans have
made higher education accessible to millions of young people who, in
most countries, simply would not have found it possible. In the 1980s
these programs have been cut back sharply along with other social programs on the theory that those who are highly motivated will still find it
possible to attend some institutions of higher learning and that public
scholarship grants should be reserved for the "truly needy." It is also
argued, with some merit, that students are themselves the prime economic
beneficiaries of higher education and that they should expect to pay much
more of the cost in light of their anticipated higher earnings. When all
young people receive equal benefits regardless of need, the effect may be
a large-scale subsidy of the middle class and a diminishing of resources
available to lower classes.

But that argument could apply equally well to public school education,
and who can fail to see the benefits to the whole society of making that
freely and universally available to all. Higher education confers so many
benefits on all of us that it is a mistake to treat it as a consumption item for
which students must pay full price. The state of California reaped many
benefits from its superb system of essentially free colleges and universities in becoming one of the most creative and productive areas of economic life in the world. Substantial increases in tuition charges there in
recent years may prove to have been a public policy mistake. There may
be some merit in Boston University President John Silber's proposal of a
system of public loans available to all students which would then be repaid
on a logical and not crippling basis through the income-tax system.[12]

Whatever the form of funding, it would appear that society has a great stake in even further expansion of the principle of free access for all qualified persons to higher education.

Much could also be said about the priority of cultural development as such. Vast expansion of continuing education and adult education programs, often organized by community colleges or universities, is one of the most exciting developments in American life in recent years. It is a reminder that education is a life-long venture and that it needs to be competently organized and adequately funded to be successful. So also with other aspects of cultural life. Music, drama, visual arts, etc., are important parts of the life of the community, and they should be given high priority. There is a strong tradition in the United States—much more so than in Europe—that such aspects of cultural life should be funded through private subscription and philanthropy. In part, this insistence on private funding is in recognition of the partly private and subjective character of artistic taste and the desire to keep these things free from enforced standardization by an authoritarian government. But in part it is only one more instance of one-sided commitment to laissez-faire ideology. In any case, many communities in the United States are impoverished through the inadequacy of cultural institutions that are much weaker than their counterparts in comparable European cities. There is irony in this. Based on the fruits of free-enterprise capitalism, museums, art galleries, etc., in the U.S. often charge no admission. And some of the very finest symphony orchestras, opera and theatre companies, and art museums in the world are to be found in the great cities of the United States—despite the relative neglect of such institutions in smaller communities. We should not be too surprised. The location of quality cultural institutions is closely related to the location of concentrations of private wealth.

I have not raised this question in order to suggest that responsibility for cultural institutions should pass entirely from private to public hands, for private initiative in such spheres may have an important contribution to make. But why should a community (or a whole nation) not recognize the importance of cultural development by giving it high priority in the public budget as well? The Smithsonian Institution in Washington, D.C., illustrates the possibilities for creative interaction between public support and private initiative. One of the premier museum institutions in the world, the Smithsonian operates under quasi-public management and with public support. But it is also the beneficiary of major private philanthropies (such as the Mellon Trust) as well. Why should symphony orchestras and theatre groups in medium-sized cities (and some larger cities as well) have to struggle so much year by year to maintain their existence, while there

are so many fine musicians and actors who are unable to find adequate
employment in their preferred occupations? Is it because the musicians'
and actors' efforts are needed more in consumer production? That, if true,
might be reason enough. But what about the high unemployment rates in
Western European and North American countries? Does that not mean
that we are close to saturation so far as our employment needs are concerned in industry, and that it is time to explore other areas of community
enrichment more seriously?

As we have already noted, there was once a time when more than 90
percent of the population had to be employed in agriculture in order to
feed the community. That figure had dropped to 50 percent in the United
States by the turn of the century, and the figure today is less than 3
percent. Similarly, the proportion of the population required for industrial
labor has, in most industrialized countries, leveled off and begun to drop.
It is conceivable that industrial production could be heated up still further
in order to absorb more and more workers—but to what end? Many of the
additional increments to the national product are likely to be relatively
trivial elaborations of materialism. Would it not be better to recognize that
society is becoming increasingly liberated from material want and that the
basis now exists for giving much higher priority to those pursuits of mind
and spirit that ennoble a community? Perhaps this is what one would
expect an educator to write! But if so, it is because an educator today is
often in a position to see how many adults are hungering for opportunity
to find cultural fulfillment beyond the levels of economic necessity to
which most previous generations have been committed. And there is a
certain amount of frustration because society is not well enough organized
to accommodate and facilitate that growing desire. It can be handled
through pure private enterprise on a purely private basis, of course. But
why force the communal need onto that procrustean bed? The cultural life
of the society is largely a private matter. But it is also a public concern
and ought to be reflected among the priorities of a society as a whole
when it acts through government.

What of religious institutions and activities? This, too, can be affirmed
as among the foremost social priorities of any great society. The fundamental perspective of this book is that *all* of the defensible priorities of
society are a matter of religious concern. Ultimately, a Christian will see
these priorities as a response to the will of God. But that is no less so for
the institutions and activities of the churches themselves. These are already a high priority in the United States, with more than half the American people participating in and supporting church institutions and activities. In Europe there is greater state support of religious institutions,

accompanied, usually, by much less popular participation. Some supporters of the American tradition of "separation of church and state" are inclined to attribute the greater institutional involvement of American churchgoers to this separation—and there is something to be said for it. Private support for religious institutions does tend to foster greater commitment and participation, although there are other variables involved here, such as the pluralistic history of American religion and the cultural effects of two bloody world wars fought on the European continent. In any case, I would not suggest inclusion of religion among the budgetary priorities of the U.S. government. Aside from obvious constitutional problems, that priority is being attended to appropriately and well on the present basis. It does seem wise, however, for society to protect the opportunity for churches to function economically. Dean Kelley makes a convincing case for church exemption from many taxes[13] although this is an indirect form of public subsidy. Churches should also have access to the channels of public communication, with due respect being paid to the religious pluralism of the community.

This chapter has only scratched the surface of the implications and possibilities of a full-employment policy. I have sought to stress two underlying points: first, that employment of some kind is a right and need of everybody if they are to be what God intends people to be; and second, that it is a mistake to trust the free market by itself to attend to this need adequately. Much, probably most, employment can be handled through private institutions in the Western mixed-economy systems. But the public sector is important in managing the whole and in ensuring the availability of work and educational opportunity for all. Private initiative and communal decision-making through the political process are both important.

CHAPTER EIGHT

Priority Four: Conservation

Some years ago, when the Environmental Protection Agency of the United States had just begun its work of curtailing pollution of the nation's atmosphere and waterways, the steel industry in an Ohio river valley was confronted by the awful mess it had made of the river. For many years the river had served as a sewerage system for the steel mills into which they had routinely dumped their waste products. The mills had profited handsomely by thus economically solving their waste problem. They had persuaded many of the workers that their jobs and the prosperity of the valley depended on being able to continue this practice, even though the river had become an unhealthy eyesore. Threatened by new governmental regulation, the industry organized a citizens' group to fight this infringement of the "sacred" right to dispose of pollutants in the public domain. The dispute attracted some national attention. One evening the chairperson of the citizens' organization was interviewed on national television. Watching the interview, I was fascinated to hear this man draw a distinction between "recreational rivers" and "working rivers." The river valley in question was, he said, a "working" river.

By that standard, much of the environment of industrial societies has been a "working" environment! Industry, unrestrained by anything but market forces, has often laid waste the rivers and atmosphere and forests and fields as though these things were nothing but resources for the industrial enterprise. The biosphere and the teeming varieties of life with which we share this planet have been treated with disregard in the absence of external restraints generated by an aroused community. In Europe this issue was faced much earlier than it was in North America, although pollution is far from unknown on the European continent even today. In the United States and Canada, land was plentiful, population relatively sparse, and resources seemingly unlimited. In time, however, the growth of industry and the waste of resources and environment came to threaten the quality of life of the whole society. Community response to this challenge occurred in the United States in two historical periods. The first was the "Progressive Era" of the first two decades of this century. National parks and forests were established, along with other notable conservation efforts. The second was the ecology movement of the 1970s, when the conservation effort achieved maximum public support and public commitment was translated into landmark legislation and programs. The 1980s have witnessed some retreats from this commitment in the United States— some of which were symbolized by the leadership of Secretary James Watt in the Interior Department. But it is clear from all the electoral campaigns of the 1980s that serious neglect of the environment and resources of the nation remains very unpopular.

The Moral Reality of Conservation

The conservation movement of the 1970s was accompanied by much serious theological and ethical reflection.[1] Biblical exegetes pointed out the implications of the creation stories of Genesis, including the distinction between aspects of those accounts that emphasized and gave license to human dominance of the earth and those that saw humanity as playing a stewardship role, with responsibility before God for the preservation of the beauties as well as the utilities of the earth. Humanity may have a kind of authority over the world. But, if so, that authority is not license to destroy it. Recent theological reflection has recovered the notion that the world was not created simply for the sake of human beings. Whatever the special character of men and women in the divine scheme of things, it is not as though humanity were all that matters. Everything else is also special to God.

Even if humanity were all that mattered or matters most, the moral reality of conservation involves the relationship of people of one generation with those of all other generations. The world into which we are born is our legacy from the past. The world as we leave it is our legacy for future generations. The moral reality as it is seen in a theological way is that we are a part of the same moral community with those of past and future times. One can therefore agree with the emphasis placed by the Nairobi Assembly of the World Council of Churches on the *sustainability* of society.[2] Not only are we to be concerned about "justice" and "participation," but we must also care whether society can continue into the indefinite future.

The urgency of that priority can be underscored in purely humanistic as well as theological terms. Seen in an entirely humanistic sense, future generations represent the only sustaining meaning our lives can have. It is only as our descendants are able to bear the meaning of our accomplishments that those accomplishments will be registered beyond the few years we can live on earth. The authentic humanistic response to Robert Heilbroner's flippant question, "what has posterity ever done for me?"[3] is that it has given people some degree of objective immortality. That is at least a deeper, more commendable form of humanism than the have-it-all-now, we-only-live-once variety. Those who see reality in theological terms, with God as the source and meaning and sustaining basis of all that is, have all the more reason to take a responsible attitude toward the world and future generations.

Either a humanistic or a theological attitude makes clear that economics must be conducted as though people were not the only thing that mattered and as though the present generation were not the last one. Economic life must be structured in such a way that short-term interests are not allowed to crowd out long-run priorities. Great corporations, particularly those with some tradition and character, take a strategic view of the future. They are not as likely to allow questions of short-term profitability to extinguish prospects for future well-being. I have already noted the problem that market forces, taken by themselves, create incentives for short-term goals over long-term ones. But great corporations are often able to transcend those market forces, at least to a considerable extent. The problem is that even the most visionary corporation is not likely to be governed with a single eye toward the long-run good of all society. Sustainability must be everybody's business.

The Difficult Trade-Offs

How simple this would all be if it were just a matter of convincing ourselves and others that we should conserve the environment and resources for the future! The best way to do this might be to eliminate industry altogether and return to the simpler modes of agriculture and hunting and fishing. Some rhetoricians of the ecology movement almost imply that such simplicity is both possible and desirable.

The conservation priority, however, can be on a collision course with other economic priorities. The production of adequate food, clothing, and shelter and the provision of adequate heat and light and transportation—not to mention the provision of labor-saving devices and other amenities—requires expenditure of energy and resources. The energy has to come from somewhere, and many energy sources have polluting byproducts. In the main, the Industrial Revolution was powered by fossil fuels. The burning of coal and petroleum, in particular, made modern industry and transportation possible. Without the Industrial Revolution, the present world population of about 4.8 billion people is scarcely imaginable. Which means that the present world population probably could not be sustained without substantial continued reliance on fossil fuels. But those fuels exist in finite quantities, and their use, while they last, clearly disrupts the world environment.

The basic dilemma is illustrated very well in many Third World settings. Eager to gain the benefits of industrial technologies for their burgeoning and impoverished populations, many Third World leaders regard the ecology movement as a luxury they can ill afford. They are prepared to accept more pollution if that is what is required to meet the basic needs of their people. The results can be tragic. The magnificent beauty of the high plateau of Mexico City, surrounded by a crown of snow-capped mountains, is now enshrouded in a blanket of smog. The great city of Bogotá is but dimly visible from the high Andes Mountains against which it nestles. The million citizens of Ibadan, Nigeria, live daily with suffocating congestion. The streams of such countries reek with the waste of industrial activity. But without that activity, it appears that the economies of those countries could not possibly sustain present population levels, and it is difficult to find anybody in the Third World who wishes to return to the simple primitive life styles of the past. There is no easy answer to this trade-off. Difficult choices have to be made, balancing off the benefits of given levels of production against given levels of pollution and given rates of depletion of natural resources.

Conservative writers like the Friedmans, Novak, and Gilder who are generally antagonistic to governmental regulation are quite correct in observing that regulations prohibiting particular forms of pollution or attempting to enforce conservation of resources do not come without costs. Often the bearers of the costs are unaware of them, and sometimes those who bear the costs are not the prime beneficiaries of the regulations. The Friedmans argue this last point:

> The problem of controlling pollution and protecting the environment is greatly complicated by the tendency for the gains and losses derived from doing so to fall on different people. The people, for example, who gain from the greater availability of wilderness areas, or from the improvement of the recreational quality of lakes and rivers, or from the cleaner air in the cities, are generally not the same people as those who would lose from the resulting higher costs of food or steel or chemicals. Typically, we suspect, the people who would benefit most from the reduction of pollution are better off, financially and educationally, than the people who would benefit most from the lower cost of things that would result from permitting more pollution.[4]

Whether that is true in a given instance comes down to factual details. The crippling of a productive industry employing thousands for the sake of relatively marginal conservationist gains might be one thing, and the crippling of an environment or a resource future for the sake of marginal production and employment benefits might be quite another. There must be large numbers of long-term employees in the asbestos industry who wish some government agency had been much more thorough in its research and regulation so that they could have known at the outset the potential health hazards. It would be difficult to put the risk of the snail darter in the construction of the Tennessee Valley Authority's Tellico Dam—with all its potential economic benefits—in quite the same light. In retrospect, the worst fears of the conservationists about the Alaska oil-pipeline project never materialized, while the economic benefits of the project have been considerable. On the other hand, the political pressures mounted insistently by the conservationists may well have been what kept the project in balance with the environment.

It is not always easy to make these determinations. We can err either in the direction of unnecessarily hobbling needed economic production or of endangering the environment, the public health, or the future supply of basic resources.

The question is, Who is to decide? Milton Friedman, to his credit, acknowledges that there are situations where government must supersede the market mechanism in assessing costs and determining priorities. When the "neighborhood effect" is encountered—that is, when the actions of some inevitably affect the well-being of all and the market is unable to assign costs and benefits in the usual way—then government must assume responsibility.[5] He is undoubtedly right in that judgment, though such situations probably arise much more frequently than he supposes. Many things affect the physical quality of life of the whole community. It is very difficult for the market mechanism to provide a rational way for consumers to indicate their preferences about the overall state of the environment when it is in competition with jobs and consumer goods. I might prefer to buy and drive an automobile without antipollution devices because it would be cheaper to buy in the first place, and it would give better gas mileage, and it would run on regular gasoline that is cheaper than lead-free gasoline. If I could drive such a car while everybody else used cars with pollution devices, my car would not measurably affect the common environment. I could have my cake and eat it. But, while my decision as a consumer can affect my purchase, it cannot determine others. Even if I am a responsible citizen and make a purchase that is in harmony with the overall environmental needs of the community, others might do otherwise, and I would lose both the economic benefits of the cheaper car and the desired environmental benefits. There has to be decision-making by the community as such, and not just the sum total of individual consumer decisions.

Acknowledging this, Friedman nevertheless urges that needed governmental controls be done by assigning fees to offset the presumed economic benefits from environmentally unsound practices, both to act as an economic (rather than punitive) deterrent to the practices and to provide the funds to offset the damages. In many cases, he argues, this would make it easier to determine what the actual costs of conservation measures are by observing the behavior of the polluters and resource users at different levels of fees.[6] There may be something to that.

I suspect, on the other hand, that there are instances where tight regulatory control, with serious legal enforcement, may be needed. That is particularly true where the basic health and well-being of people is on the line. In a way, the market system is involved in product safety and toxic waste–disposal systems—for those who have been injured by industrial decisions can sue and receive substantial damages in civil court. But, as a matter of personal and community well-being, who can put a price tag on ruined health and premature mortality and say, after the fact, that fair compensation has been rendered? The more complex modern industry and society become the more necessary it is to have public watchdogs on duty—with teeth as well as with the ability to bark and growl!

Who Speaks for the Future?

Earlier we raised the question of sustainability. How, really, are we to deal with the trade-offs involved when present economic benefits seem to be in conflict with future well-being? Recent conservative writers tend to approach the problem with two stock answers: First, disputing the views of the Club of Rome and other "alarmist" writings, they may question whether present patterns of production and consumption really do threaten future well-being as much as is alleged.[7] Second, questioning the need for or value of governmental planning, they will argue that the free market is precisely the mechanism that will come up with solutions to future problems as it has to those of the past. For instance, the Industrial Revolution was initially powered by water, then by steam—with wood and coal as heat-generating fuels. Alarmism about diminishing coal resources would have been quite premature, since petroleum was about to be harnessed to internal combustion engines and discovered in great quantities worldwide. Similarly, the projected ultimate loss of fossil fuels (coal and petroleum) at some point in the foreseeable future will make it increasingly costly to use those fuels and increasingly feasible economically for private enterprise to do the research and development needed for alternative energy sources.

There is some truth to this. But applied to really important economic questions, this faith in future inventiveness remains a conjecture based on a fairly limited base of historical experience. The fact that unforeseen inventions and discoveries in the past have occurred in time to save people from the effects of waste and depletion is no guarantee that this will always happen in the future. It is a very risky thing to assume that laissez-faire will always evoke the creativity to solve the problems that laissez-faire has created. Farmlands and forests have been turned into deserts, and then they have stayed deserts. Resources have been depleted, and then they have been gone. People have sickened and died as a result of misguided relationships with the natural environment, and their loss has been beyond repair. Whole species have become extinct and gone forever.[8]

Humanity, obviously, has not been one of those species. Far from it, people have done very well in their few millions of years on earth. And the Industrial Revolution has in fact created conditions enabling a dramatic population explosion to occur—with world population increasing more than threefold in the twentieth century alone. Nevertheless, this is no guarantee of the future. The very suddenness of recent industrial developments should give us pause in assessing the future. The pace of change should lead to greater humility in our forecasting. The past dozen years or so have brought forth a very large chorus of alarmism, to be matched in turn by voices of reassurance and optimism. The striking thing about the First Global Conference on the Future (Toronto, 1980), apart from its pretentious title, was the utter incongruity of its mixture of alarmists and reassurers, optimists and pessimists, ecologists and technologists—all claiming exclusive wisdom in their visions of the future.[9]

Whom should we trust to represent the future? If the alarmists and pessimists are right, we had better give the conservation agenda a very high priority in our economic and political planning. If the technologists and reassuring optimists are right, we can get on with other things and let the future attend to itself. The future itself, unfortunately, cannot speak.

Conservation as a Priority

We have already registered the point that we belong to the same moral community as future generations and that we are responsible to God and to them for their well-being. We have also sought to be clear that the world is more than a human preserve and that nature is more than a facility for human well-being, inseparable though the welfare of humanity and the rest of nature may ultimately be.

But what specific guidance can be given when the conservation agenda appears to clash with other priorities? The present and future well-being of billions of people depends on the adequacy of economic production. When technological development appears necessary for all those people while at the same time it seems to pose a threat to the environment and the future, we have a real dilemma on our hands. Resources that are devoted to conservation cannot be used for direct human consumption, at least not most of the time. So choices have to be made.

I wish to suggest two principles for resolving such dilemmas.

First, we need to take into account the relative degree of importance of the specific claims of present vs. future and humanity vs. nature. When the basic existence and humanness of our contemporaries is at stake, it seems reasonable to sacrifice a good many environmental concerns of lesser importance. On the other hand, when fundamental environmental dangers are threatened, it does not seem reasonable to subordinate them to trivial human luxuries and pleasures. (By that standard, I think the advent of supersonic jet transportation to save rich passengers two or three hours transatlantic flight time was a bad bargain, given its high consumption of jet fuel and effect on the earth's ozone layers.) Sometimes the trade-offs are more evenly balanced and the dilemmas more difficult. But when one side of the equation is clearly more trivial than the other, the choice of priority should be equally clear.

The second principle is that uncertainties about the seriousness of specific interventions in the natural environment should be resolved conservatively until we are clear that our actions will not lead to catastrophe. The burden of proof should have to be met by actions having a major environmental impact, not the other way around. That should be true in any case, but it is particularly so given the present pace of change. It is so easy for us to overshoot the mark before we realize what we have done. That is not to inhibit all material progress; it is to test in advance those developments with large potential impact. It is too bad we did not know more about the carcinogenic effects of asbestos before it was used, on a large scale, in the construction of ceiling materials in public buildings and schools. It is too bad we did not realize that excessive exposure to X-rays can lead to leukemia before frequent X-ray treatments were used to relieve comparatively minor arthritic problems. It is too bad we did not anticipate the effects of industrial processes in causing "acid rain." But we have had enough experience, now, in coping with the unintended but serious effect of "progress" to establish caution as a principle. [10] Caution often proves unnecessary and, in retrospect, can even be ridiculed. Lack of sufficient caution, however, can lead to disaster. When the stakes are high and there is substantial uncertainty, we need to be more conservative than we have often been.

Laissez-faire economics has been a factor for only the last couple of centuries, and it can hardly be blamed for all of the shortsighted, risky practices of the past. But the attitude that immediate gain need alone concern us or that the self-correcting mechanisms of economic life will save us from our folly is a spirit shared by many capitalist writers of our time. There are, as a matter of fact, many socialists who also hold the same illusions.[11] But neither capitalist nor socialist versions of letting the future take care of itself will do. Every generation presents a legacy to the future of good or ill. Even with the best intentions we can make serious mistakes; how much greater the risks when we blunder ahead as though we were incapable of damaging the natural world and future generations fundamentally. The future cannot act or speak for itself today except as it does so through the mind and will of farsighted people who care about the generations yet to come.

CHAPTER NINE

Priority Five: A New World Order

> *At the beginning of a new decade, only twenty years*
> *short of the millennium, we must try to lift ourselves*
> *above day-to-day quarrels (or negotiations) to see*
> *the menacing long-term problems. We see a world in*
> *which poverty and hunger still prevail in many huge*
> *regions; in which resources are squandered without*
> *consideration of their renewal; in which more arma-*
> *ments are made and sold than ever before; and*
> *where a destructive capacity has been accumulated*
> *to blow up our planet several times over. There is no*
> *reasonable alternative to a policy of reducing ten-*
> *sions and bringing about a higher degree of cooper-*
> *ation.*
>
> —Willy Brandt (1980)[1]

These words by former West German Chancellor Willy Brandt introduced the celebrated Brandt Commission Report on international development issues. This widely read document was enthusiastically applauded by
some and roundly condemned by others, usually on the basis of particular
recommendations contained within the report. The title of the report,
North–South, suggested a framing of world problems by reference to the
relationship between the richer industrial countries of the Northern hemi-
sphere and the poorer Third World countries of the South. The report did
emphasize that relationship. But the deeper meaning of the report was its
sense of global community. Economic and political issues should no
longer be seen in purely national terms. We all belong to the same world.
Everybody's business should become everybody's business.

That is not hard to agree with in Christian theological terms. This is,
after all, God's world. The earth is still the Lord's "and the fulness
thereof." Morally we all belong together as to a single family. Even if this
were not so, the practical realities of the world of the late twentieth cen-

115

tury remind us every day of our interdependence with people of remote places whom we will never meet face to face. A recognition of our relationships with others seems increasingly important to mutual survival and well-being in a world rent by conflict and plagued by problems that know no national boundaries. Pope John XXIII made the moral and practical point at the same time in his encyclical *Pacem In Terris* when he spoke of the need for a new world order: "at this historical moment the present system of organization and the way its principle of authority operates on a world basis no longer correspond to the objective requirements of the universal common good."[2]

The moral imperative and practical urgency of acting on the basis of global consciousness are understood by more and more people. But it is very difficult to translate this into priorities and policies, particularly in economics. The basic structure of political economy is national. It is at the national level that currency is managed, taxes are determined, trade is regulated, efforts are made to control cyclical fluctuations and to deal with poverty, and property rights are ultimately defined and secured. Socialist countries may lay claim to greater sensitivity to social justice, but their behavior in the contemporary world can be quite as nationalistic as the capitalists'—sometimes more so. We may all respond with generosity to the latest famine in Africa or Asia or to the latest earthquake in Latin America. But economics is institutionalized along national lines.

Getting out of this box should itself be a high priority. It will not be easy. Self-interest is often derived from national interest, and national interest can be defined as the sum of the private interests of those making up the nation. Even those who benefit least from nationalism may be most devoted to it. Religiously speaking, this can be idolatrous, and it can be a particularly attractive form of idolatry during a period of cultural and spiritual crisis such as our own. Even those who approach the nation without religious fervor can find nationalism a convenient way to protect and enhance their own material interests.[3] The combination of idolatrous nationalism with individual self-interest creates an even more powerful obstacle to world consciousness.

Still, one may record that that consciousness is developing. On a practical level, the vast increases in planetary communication and travel and trade render the nationalistic spirit more and more inconvenient and embarrassing. Our situation may be a little like the late medieval world when the parochial spirit was still very strong but the inconveniences of archaic feudal boundaries were felt with growing impatience. One may also note evidence of spiritual oneness, as in the response by large numbers of people to human need in remote areas of the earth, made visible and immediate by television. That spirit has had to face grave setbacks in the fanatic group loyalties and murderous conflicts of some parts of the world; but still it grows. In spite of the idolatries and the cynicisms of our time, there are very many people who recognize, in faith, that they are a part of a universal human family.

How can we give economic substance and foundation to this recognition so that in our economic life we do not have to live in self-contradiction on the world level? I wish to suggest three points at which we are challenged to think beyond national boundaries and act toward the creation of a new world order. Each of these has very important implications for economic policy.

Overcoming the Gap Between
Rich and Poor Nations

Poverty, as we have seen in chapter 4, is a global as well as national reality. The gulf between rich and poor nations is enormous and, in relative terms, growing. Taking note of this, most of the developing nations have banded together to demand the creation of a New International Economic Order (NIEO). Their proposals emphasize improvements in terms of trade, higher prices for the commodities they produce, sharing of technology, easier credit terms. They demand this not only as a matter of simple justice but as a practical prerequisite to further development of those trade relationships on which the wealthier countries have also come to depend.

Critics of the NIEO demands have been quick to point out flaws. Predictably, the more ideological advocates of free enterprise have said that free trade and a political climate conducive to business investment will alone provide the key to overcoming the poverty of Third World countries. Not so predictably, the NIEO proposals were criticized by those with a deeper commitment to social justice. Two such critics, for example, wrote that "we believe the call for a new international economic order by the leaders of the Third World is a sham and a fraud designed to divert the attention of their people from the internal structures that block development, keep the people poor, and perpetuate hunger, disease, and illiteracy."[4] They may have a point. Justice for Paraguay or Guatemala does not necessarily mean justice for the Paraguayans or Guatemalans. It may only mean that elites in such countries get richer, while the poor get nothing.

Still, the problem of relationships between rich and poor lands remains. Is it not morally intolerable that half the world's population should live in utter destitution while others enjoy very great prosperity? If North Americans or Europeans or Japanese think of social justice only in national terms, they can do much to erase poverty from their midst. But poverty will continue to be a stark reality in global terms. Moreover, wealthy countries will always have to live insecurely as long as they are surrounded by the increasingly resentful poor.

There is nothing new about all this, of course. In thinking about the chasm between the poor and the prosperous, our tendency is either to become increasingly callous or to be spiritually immobilized by guilt. Christians, despite the centrality of their gospel of grace, can be as prone to play on one another's sense of guilt as any other people. In fact, however, it is very difficult to assign specific blame for what has been termed the "predicament of the prosperous"[5] in face of the immensity of global poverty. Guilt and blame are almost beside the point. The point is to try to deal with the objective circumstances of global poverty as best we can.

But what is to be done?

Those who care most about these things must be struck by the radical divergence of diagnosis and prescription. Capitalists call for free markets and free trade, while Marxists call for revolution. Foreign-aid advocates call for rich nations to tax themselves 1 percent of their Gross National Product in order to provide direct development grants and loans for poor nations, while NIEO supporters call for redress in trade relationships. Some continue to speak of getting poor nations to the developmental "takeoff" point where they can continue economic growth on their own, while others decry the large-scale visions of most developmental strategies in the name of more labor-intensive intermediate technologies. Many of the proposals seem absolutely inconsistent with alternative ideas, yet all are put forth with impressive supporting data. Why the disagreements, why so many competing solutions?

In part it is certainly because there are ideological axes being ground. Marxists and capitalists are bound to diagnose the realities of wealth and poverty in Marxist and capitalist terms—and to prescribe solutions accordingly. Both correctly perceive that important long-range power interests hinge on how poverty within and beyond nations is diagnosed and treated. In light of the ideological perspectives and the interests at stake, it is not surprising that one would emphasize data supporting one's views while overlooking facts that do not.

But conflicting views of world poverty also have something to do with the sheer size and diversity of the world. Depending on one's definition, sixty or eighty countries can be classified as being in the Third World, and these countries, while poor, are very different from one another. Dependency theory, which attributes the underdevelopment of poor countries to the development—and exploitation—by rich countries,[6] may very well describe some of the Latin American countries along with some other situations, but it hardly explains contemporary China or Chad or Ethiopia. The free market/free trade solution might characterize the recent development of Hong Kong, Taiwan, or South Korea—but it has not done much for Haiti or Liberia. The socialist development model can claim modest but real economic success in China and Cuba, but its track record in Mozambique and Kampuchea is an embarrassment. Petroleum deposits seem to help, drought to hinder; culture and history also matter. Really bad leaders can set the development process back for decades—as illustrated in Argentina, Ghana, and Haiti—while really good ones can help move things along against all the odds—almost regardless of ideology. Population growth rates often make a difference.

In light of this diversity and confusion, what can Europeans and North Americans *do* to make a difference? How can this become an effective priority in our economic thinking and policy formation? I have no panaceas to offer, but there is something to be said for each of the following points:

First, we have already emphasized the importance of global consciousness. We need to remember that attitudes matter and that direct contact with poverty can affect attitudes. Public and private programs increasing human contact and communication are likely to be helpful in energizing people for the tasks of overcoming global poverty. There are, no doubt, serious flaws in most of the development programs that have been attempted in recent decades. And yet one can be struck by the effect of such programs in heightening awareness and involvement of people who can often learn from their mistakes and improve their performance. The American Peace Corps, for instance, was easily and rightly subject to criticism: young people naively approaching problems whose histories and complexities they could scarcely imagine. But the Peace Corps volunteers also brought a degree of caring and enthusiasm to their work that helped other people care and be enthusiastic, and on their return to the United States they helped increase the global awareness of others. Caring and enthusiasm are still badly needed; pessimism and cynicism about the world can be its most deadly enemies.

Second, the need continues for generous transfer grants from prosperous to poor countries. Economists of all persuasions seem to regard the development of economic surplus (beyond what is needed to sustain basic subsistence farming) as necessary for movement into industrial production and world trade. Some Third World countries are blessed with oil as a source for this surplus, though most are not. The classic approach, whether in England or Germany or Russia or China, has been to acquire that surplus through the incredible exertions and sacrifices (often involuntary) of at least one generation of workers and peasants. It is still possible for most developing countries to achieve economic success by sacrificing a generation or two of their people, although political conditions now make this much more difficult apart from authoritarian leadership and military rule. An important alternative is for wealthier countries to make capital available through grants and loans. I will be reminded by some readers that private investment does the same thing, which it certainly does under optimal conditions. But much of the world is unwilling to allow control of its economic development to drift into the hands of First World corporations, and the economic role of the public sector is central in many Third World countries. Aid and loan programs have not always been successful. Sometimes they have been ill fitted to local conditions. Sometimes they have contributed to corruption. Sometimes developing countries have been saddled with long-term debts for projects from which no return has been realized.

Still, rather than abandoning foreign-assistance programs, we should learn more from previous successes and failures. Foreign-assistance grants and loans need to be sound economically, implemented with discipline, and as detached from political interests as possible. Their effect should be to broaden the base of employment in the recipient country and not to provide disproportionate income and wealth to the officials administering them.

How generous should the aid programs of the prosperous countries be? The widely acknowledged though seldom implemented standard of 1 percent of a country's annual GNP has much to be said for it. (For the United States, with a GNP in excess of $3 trillion, the standard would come to something above $30 billion.) That could include funds for loans and direct grants, though not for military purposes. While $30 billion per year may seem like an enormous amount of money, it is not much more than 10 percent of the current military budget of the United States. Well-targeted economic aid might very well be the better investment in the nation's security in the long run!

Third, it is best to provide aid through multilateral agreements and agencies as much as possible. Aid programs dispensed through international agencies, such as the World Bank, can best circumvent local political pressures and keep the recipient nations accountable. Individual countries, like the United States, West Germany, and Great Britain, might lose some specific political leverage in the process, but what really matters is whether recipient countries are getting on with development. If they are, the net long-term effect is likely to be the kind of world in which we can all be safer and more prosperous. Moreover, the strengthening of a world development regime is probably desirable in itself. We are a long way from being able to think seriously about world government, particularly in light of the continuing East-West conflict. But international economic institutions with substantial economic power could be a major step in the right direction.

The fourth point is that specific attention needs to be given to the enormous debt currently carried by many Third World countries, such as Argentina, Mexico, and Brazil. Debt service, in several instances, now eats up the precious foreign exchange credits earned by some countries, making it almost impossible for them to get on with the development task. In 1983 the total outstanding debt of the developing countries came to $595.8 billion, which represented 26.7 percent of those countries' Gross National Product. This was an increase from $68.4 billion in 1970, which was 13.3 percent of their GNP.[7] Some of the borrowing was for projects whose economic returns were overestimated, in which cases interest payments are a little like having to continue to make mortgage payments on a house that burned down without insurance. Some of the economic returns on the borrowing will not be realized for many years, though the long-term benefits may well be worth the costs of the loans. (That includes the development of basic energy sources and transport systems, important preconditions to other forms of production and marketing.) In some instances the benefits of economic development have been engulfed in a too-high population growth rate that places heavy demands on institutions and services.

Besides improving the quality of future loans and grants, the international community needs to give special attention to assisting many developing countries in their short-term obligations, refinancing some and canceling others.[8]

Fifth, the principle of international ownership of the deep seabeds, Antarctica, accessible outer space, etc., with realizable benefits being used by the community of nations for developmental purposes, is both wise economics and visionary politics (as well as good theology). The Law of the Sea Treaty's presupposition that the deep seabeds are the "common heritage" of humankind is a principle that should be extended into other areas—and it should be accepted and ratified by the government of the United States, which, until now, it has not been. It may be too early to think of overall global management of economic life. But it is not too early for the international community to acquire experience in economic management, as indeed it already has in the imperfect procedures of the International Monetary Fund, among other things.

The gap between rich and poor nations will continue into the foreseeable future, but it should be a very high priority of economic policy to take every available step to close it. Strengthening of international development institutions with increased power and more generous levels of funding can provide a basis for energizing hope among the poor nations of the world. The process is bound to be uneven, given the great diversity of situations to which development strategies apply; and there will be disappointments and frustrations in the future as there have been in the past. But people of good will can accomplish a great deal one step at a time.

The Regulation of Multinational Corporations

Over the past dozen years or so a considerable debate has erupted over the growing prominence of multinational (or transnational) corporations. Alternatively they are praised or damned. To some they represent the real hope for economic development in a coming world community; these corporations are substantially international institutions and they are spreading their investments and developing new markets everywhere. To others they embody irresponsible capitalism at its worst, with accountability to no single nation or to the community of nations as a whole. Some see them as peculiarly vulnerable to the whims of a hundred governments in a hundred places, forced to be unusually scrupulous because of their unusually high visibility. Some, quite to the contrary, see them as being able to force their will on relatively weak national governments and to hoodwink the relatively strong ones. The literature of the 1970s and '80s has catalogued the horror stories as well as celebrated the benefits of this important phenomenon.[9]

Multinational corporations are hardly new. Indeed, in a certain sense the very first corporations were multinational. But their importance has blossomed impressively in the post–World War II era, with particular development in the last dozen years or so. Some critics—including some church social-action leaders—have treated multinational corporations as a force that should be opposed and, if possible, abolished. But that seems like an excessive reaction for two good reasons: first, because they are plainly well established for a long time to come, and second, because many of them are performing useful functions in a number of countries. The most sweeping case to be made against them depends heavily on some form of dependency theory or Marxist analysis. I find it interesting that there are even some Marxists who consider the historic role of the MNCs in developing the world's technological base to be a useful though transitional function.[10] In any event, like it or not, they are here to stay for a long time.

But it is not foreordained that their role will be constructive. We have already noted the paradox of the unregulated free market in rewarding unethical behavior insofar as it is cost-effective. Within a single country governmental regulations can bring private economic factors to heel when necessary, especially if the country is strong and has a diversified economic life. Thus, corporations can be compelled to adopt safety standards, to pay minimum wages, to recognize labor unions, to refrain from polluting air and water, to observe specified restraints in their marketing practices, and so on. All the great industrial countries have acquired considerable experience in regulating economic activity so that the market rewards will not flow easily toward the least scrupulous.

But that is much more difficult for weak, underdeveloped countries. A small country may be disproportionately dependent on a few major corporations, and those corporations may have quite enough economic power to pull out of what they take to be unpleasant situations. Great transnational corporations may also be adept in manipulating local politics through timely largess to strategically placed politicians and voters.

The U.N. Center for Transnational Corporations has begun to exert some countervailing influence here, for it has made it possible for small nations to band together in confronting corporate giants while also providing those countries with needed information about the corporations and with tested techniques for regulating their behavior. In some areas, such as international communications and aviation, the international community has acquired considerable experience in dealing with transnational business activity. But these are areas where it is obviously in everybody's interest, the companies included, for universal rules to apply. The regulation of most competitive business behavior is, at the international level, still in its infancy. The U.N. center is one promising venture, the 1981 World Health Organization's Code of Marketing of Breastmilk Substitutes (to govern the marketing practices of infant-formula companies) is another, the Law of the Sea Treaty is a third.

The establishment of a fabric of international regulation should be an important priority for economic policy in our time. It is especially important for the more vulnerable countries; but in the long run it also seems in the interest of the corporations themselves. Regulation of marketing practices, employment policies, waste-disposal techniques, productive safety, and so on, is a protection for those business leaders of good will who do not want to be placed at a competitive disadvantage by being socially responsible. It is also a defense against unfair criticism and sudden expropriation for their business ventures to be regularized in socially acceptable ways.

The infant-formula controversy of the 1970s and 1980s illustrates the value of international regulatory standards. The Nestlé Company and several large U.S. multinational corporations engaged in selling infant formula in the Third World came under severe criticism for their use of marketing techniques leading to unhealthy uses of the product by the Third World mothers, most of whom should breast-feed their infants. The U.S. companies were subjected to much public criticism, and Nestlé became the object of a widespread economic boycott. While conducting hearings on the controversy in 1978, U.S. Sen. Edward Kennedy proposed that the World Health Organization and UNICEF help develop a framework of understanding for acceptable marketing behavior in that industry. The idea was pursued and, in 1981, the World Health Assembly adopted a code of marketing. The code provided a norm to which companies could be held by their critics; but it also helped check excessive criticism. At length, Nestlé agreed to abide by the code, and other companies began to follow suit.[11]

Whatever the self-correcting mechanisms of democratic capitalist society may be, they depend on the existence of some governing authority to establish and maintain the rules of the game, to protect the vulnerable and assure economic stability. That authority exists, though imperfectly, within democratic nations. Unfortunately, it scarcely exists at all at the world level. But it is at the global level that the most dramatic new developments in economic life occur. The development of some kind of governing authority to discipline multinational corporations is clearly in the interest of all of us, including the corporations themselves.

World Peace and Disarmament

World peace is not exactly something we can go out and buy, but it must be our highest global priority—particularly when it is combined with a tolerable level of social justice. Twentieth-century humanity has had to rely on an uneasy balance of power among nations to preserve the peace, and the bloody history of this century amply demonstrates the failure of that system. The post–World War II period has witnessed an uneasy stand-off between the United States and the USSR, both of whom rely on gigantic military buildups to deter aggression from each other. For many years each has had enough nuclear explosives to destroy the other many times over, and possibly to annihilate the rest of the world in the process.

Has this deterrence worked? It can be argued that it has. The two superpowers have not, in fact, made war on each other despite the many provocations and counterprovocations. And it is arguable that their mutual restraint owes more to mutual fear than to the pure love of peace—for both countries have meanwhile engaged in other wars under less perilous circumstances. Indeed, it can be said that the balance of terror between the superpowers has merely made the world safe for many small wars. It has not secured a new era of peace. This has been one of the more wretched periods of mortal combat in human history, and the conflicts show no signs of abating.[12]

There is a widespread impression, obviously shared in high places, that the road to peace and security is paved with military preparedness. Both superpowers, emulated by many less powerful nations, plainly regard military parity with potential adversaries as the basis for security. Everybody has accepted uncritically the principle that "those who would have peace must first prepare for war." There is some truth in the principle, for absolute unpreparedness does invite aggression in this fallen world! But there is also a flaw in the principle, at least as it is applied in the current arms race. Every round of increased preparedness on one side is an incentive to similar increases on the other side. Each round expands the potential order of destructiveness and in the end makes everyone more and more vulnerable to a war caused by miscalculation or accident. And meantime, the vast expansions of the world's arsenals provide ever more deadly weaponry for the smaller-scale wars and revolutions and repressions that have become almost an everyday affair. Who would dare to argue that the world is a safer, more secure place than it was when this awful arms race began four decades ago? Who supposes that the national interests of Americans, Soviets, British, French, etc., are less vulnerable than they were then? Who can rationally believe that those interests—and the interests of the rest of humankind—will be more secure after the next round of military buildups than they are even today?

But what is to be done? Unilateral disarmament, though advocated by pacifists, is not a solution to most of the rest of us. Arms-control negotiations have been fitful and easily criticized as political-power maneuvering. Realists wonder whether there is any practical alternative to present policies. But two lines of approach can be pursued that connect the problem to the main theme of this book. One priority can be expected to have some economic costs, while the other priority will in fact save a lot.

The first avenue is to do all we can to construct institutions of collective security. Each arms-control or disarmament agreement among the great powers is important, not only for its own sake but also as a precedent for further developments in the future. SALT II was not a perfect treaty. But for all its flaws it was, as some said, important as the basis for SALT III and SALT IV. The failure of the United States to ratify SALT II undoubtedly set the arms-control and disarmament process back several years. Quite apart from arms-reduction treaties, the forging of other kinds of international institutions helps provide precedents and foundations for real world order in the future. Serious levels of funding for international development agencies and the creation of regulatory institutions at the world level with real authority—as discussed earlier in this chapter—are highly desirable for the sake of global economic life. But such agencies are also important as foundations for a new world order in general. The present anarchy of international life cannot be overcome in a single generation. But the present generation can lay important foundations if it is willing to give this high enough priority. That will cost money and commitment, but future generations will bless us for the effort.

The other avenue toward a more secure world will actually save money: that is *to show more restraint in military spending.* One does not have to advocate unilateral disarmament to recognize the difference between adequate and inordinate levels of defense spending. It is the difference between having enough to deter aggression without seeking the kind of superiority that only prompts adversaries to want to catch up and be superior themselves. Estimates of "adequacy" will vary. But Western Europeans and North Americans need to take two points more seriously than they have in the past. On the one hand, if "adequacy" in nuclear weapons and delivery systems means the capacity to retaliate after a first strike by the adversary (presumably the USSR), then the West already has that capacity many times over. On the other hand, "adequacy" in conventional forces does not even have to represent equality or parity with a potential aggressor so long as one's capabilities are reasonably close. It is a well-known principle of military strategy that defensive forces have a natural advantage. It takes less to deter an aggressive attack than it does to mount one. Neither of these points adds up to dismantling the Western system of defense. But both suggest the wisdom of greater restraint.

Greater restraint in military spending is also profoundly important as an economic priority. Worldwide military expenditures totaled more than $600 billion annually by 1982, before the sharp increases of the last two or three years. Military spending by the United States has grown from $170 billion in 1980 to nearly $300 billion annually in the mid-1980s. Over the twenty-year period from 1960 to 1980 the military expenditures of developing countries quadrupled from $30 billion to $138 billion (in constant 1982 dollars).[13] Necessary as some military spending doubtless is, aren't these appalling figures? What does it say about a civilization that it is willing to substitute such profligate waste of resources for the meeting of basic human needs for food, clothing, shelter, medical care, education, recreation, and cultural enrichment? During the first half of the 1980s, the United States alone has devoted more than $1 trillion to military defense, with plans to spend an additional $2 trillion by 1990. The country is no more secure, but the world is less prosperous and less humane because of the enormity of this waste.

In an earlier chapter we ventured some observations about uses to which the same resources could be put. The Brandt Report similarly puts the matter of misplaced priorities dramatically with four illustrations:

1. The [world] military expenditure of only half a day would suffice to finance the whole malaria eradication programme of the World Health Organization, and less would be needed to conquer river-blindness, which is still the scourge of millions.

2. A modern tank costs about one million dollars; that amount could improve storage facilities for 100,000 tons of rice and thus save 4000 tons or more annually: more persons can live on just over a pound of rice a day. The same sum of money could provide 1000 classrooms for 30,000 children.

3. For the price of one jet fighter (20 million dollars) one could set up about 40,000 village pharmacies.

4. One-half of one percent of one year's world military expenditure would pay for all the farm equipment needed to increase food production and approach self-sufficiency in food-deficit low-income countries by 1990. [14]

Such illustrations scarcely do justice to the complexity of the problem of beating our collective swords into plowshares. But they remind us that the vastness of world military expenditures represents real priorities and that the priorities are badly misplaced and have tragic consequences. Serious efforts toward demilitarizing the world are important, both for the sake of global security and for the sake of the economic well-being of the world's people.

It might be nice if we could treat the economy and national budget of each country as a detached sphere unto itself. But the world is now an interrelated unit, and we must do our economic thinking increasingly in world and not simply national terms. At the world level the questions of economic well-being and basic security interlock in complex ways. This chapter has only scratched the surface of the important questions. But it has sought to emphasize the central point that we, particularly we who live in the rich and powerful countries, must be much more intentional about our efforts to build a world community of peace and justice with freedom and prosperity for all.

CHAPTER TEN

Saying Yes Means
Saying No

There is an especially poignant moment in Herman Wouk's novel *The Caine Mutiny*, about World War II. The novel's main character, a young naval officer named Willy Keith, has just arrived in Hawaii after being out of contact with home for several weeks. He opens and reads a letter from his father, a prosperous New York doctor. Willy is stunned to read in the letter that his father has been dying of cancer and that he is probably already dead. Through the letter Willy's father speaks of his own life as having been wasted, even though his high-income medical practice has made him wealthy. Early in his career he had made a conscious decision to "make a pile" through practicing medicine in a high-income community, even though what he had really wanted to do was pursue medical research. He had had a notion about cancer which he thought might have been an important research lead in conquering the disease. He had thought he could make his money through the rich practice and then return to the research. Now there would be no time, and his idea would die with him. His life had had its rewards, all right; there had been time for reading and golf and there had been all the creature comforts one might want. But he felt he had made the wrong choice. Pouring out his remorse, he pleaded with his son to make the right choices at those turning points when decisions must be made.[1]

We can all identify with that story because we have all made wrong choices and neglected important possibilities. In the words of the Anglican prayer of confession, "we have left undone those things we ought to have done." But the story is also a good parable about the economic situation as we have characterized it in this book. The choice of some things as priorities inevitably means the neglect of others. The first rule of economic life is that you can't have it all. Emphasize production as much as we will and should, material wants will outstrip productive capacity. Choices have to be made. If the priorities emphasized in this book are

pursued, other things will have to be deemphasized or neglected altogether. We cannot say yes to some things without saying no to others.

The great economic debate of our time is over priorities. The outcome
of the debate hinges on value commitments that are sometimes visible and
sometimes invisible, but always present. Those value commitments are
the principles of selectivity on the basis of which we decide what to say
yes to and, by implication, what we must say no to as well.

Christians are fairly well accustomed to making economic choices in
their personal and familial lives. We are usually well schooled in the
implications of the doctrine of stewardship, taken on that personal level.
We are used to hearing sermons about treating all of our material possessions as a trust from God and disposing of them wisely on the basis of that
trust. We know that we should be generous with the church and other
good causes, that we should provide for the basic needs of our families,
that we should not subordinate basics to luxuries, that our material substance should be devoted to the cultivation of life in accordance with the
overall Christian understanding of what life is all about. Often, as Christians, we oppose gambling, not because we condemn the excitement of the
game or the race or the draw, but because gambling introduces a random,
uncontrollable element into economic life that diminishes conscious decision and stewardship. Of late, many Christians have come to see the importance of greater simplicity in their personal life styles—not as an expression of antimaterial asceticism but as a way of relating more responsibly
with the natural world and of enabling greater generosity with the poor. In
short, we are used to dealing with priorities in our personal lives, and we
know that in order to say yes to some things we must say no to others.

That is true, as we have seen, for social decisions made at the level of
national and international life as well. In order to say yes to more economic benefits of a direct sort for humankind we have to say no to the vast
expansion of military spending in recent years. In order to say yes to
conservation programs that protect the future of unborn generations as
well as the quality of environmental life in the present, we may have to say
no to some forms of production and consumption, and overall GNP figures may suffer. In order to say yes to the unemployed we may have to say
no to those who equate full employment with inflation, either demonstrat-
ing that they are wrong or that (if they are right) some degree of inflation
is a price well worth paying in order to make everybody a participant in
the social enterprise. In order to say yes to the poor by expanded welfare
programs, restructured to preserve families and encourage employment,
we may have to say no to other uses of the same resources. In order to say yes
to the poor of other nations and their future we may have to say no to higher

levels of national consumption. These trade-offs need to be understood clearly and discussed frankly.

Underneath are the deep conflicts over the values by which we choose for the human venture to be led. Is individual freedom the ultimate value for us? If so, in order to say yes to freedom we shall have to say no to taxation and regulation designed to improve the overall quality of community life. If we say yes to the "opportunity society," when that term is understood to mean a society where, in Ronald Reagan's phrase, "someone can always get rich,"[2] then we shall have to say no to the more modest aspirations of many poor people. For we shall assuredly not have a society in which *all* can be rich! And as society is presently structured in most parts of the world, the riches of some have a close, though not absolute, relationship to the poverty of others. On the other hand, saying yes to absolute equality as the governing norm may mean saying no to incentives needed to encourage the extraordinary contributions of some within a society.

We have sought in these pages to emphasize the value of community life in which all are able to participate, in which all are guaranteed the material conditions necessary to their existence and participation, in which education and culture are strongly encouraged, in which there are vital and growing linkages of people throughout the world, and in which there is harmony with nature and stewardship toward the future. This view of social good does not despise individual freedom and creativity; rather it regards a high degree of personal freedom as a fundamental precondition of healthy community life. Nevertheless, saying yes to this view of social good does mean saying no to basing community life primarily on the model of competition and self-centered individualism.

Western societies have gone through convulsive changes in recent years, and many people currently are reacting against the social democratic norms that have prevailed for half a century. This reaction, to be seen in the United States, Great Britain, and elsewhere, is excessive. Saying yes to a new assertion of individual responsibility and national interest is saying no to important values of fellow feeling and global solidarity. Some of the nos now hurled at the social welfare consensus of the past half-century needed to be spoken because programs have been flawed by corruption and paternalism and many people have been deprived of opportunity to grow and mature by the very programs originally set forth to help them. But that pendulum has now swung too far. It is time for us to recover a sense of priority about the things that really matter.

Notes

Chapter One

1. Proceedings of this international symposium are published in Walter Block, Geoffrey Brennan, and Kenneth Elzinga, eds., *Morality of the Market: Religious and Economic Perspectives* (Vancouver, B.C.: The Fraser Institute, 1985).

2. While possibly underestimating the resiliency and growth potential in the American economy of the 1980s, Lester C. Thurow's *The Zero-Sum Society* (New York: Basic Books, 1980) reminded Americans that economics has to do with scarcity and that distributional problems cannot simply be solved through unlimited growth. The question he posed to political leaders on the eve of the 1980 elections was "If elected, whose income do you and your party plan to cut in the process of solving the economic problems facing us?"(p. 214). The answer of the winners, as it unfolded in the early 1980s, was that the working class and poor people would be cut out in the process of seeking to balance the federal budget and breaking the grip of inflation, while wealthier people would be given generous tax breaks in order to encourage savings and investments. Thurow was right in anticipating that there would be losers as well as winners in the economic game following the election.

3. In his essay, "Economic Possibilities for Our Grandchildren," the British economist John Maynard Keynes anticipates the time when abundance will overtake scarcity and "we shall be able to rid ourselves of many of the pseudo-moral principles which have hag-ridden us for two hundred years, by which we have exalted some of the most distasteful of human qualities into the position of the highest virtues." But, he continues, "the time for all this is not yet. For at least another hundred years we must pretend to ourselves and to every one that fair is foul and foul is fair; for foul is useful and fair is not. Avarice and usury and precaution must be our gods for a little longer still." Reprinted in J. M. Keynes, *Essays in Persuasion* (London: Macmillan & Co., 1933).

4. Lester C. Thurow, *Dangerous Currents: The State of Economics* (New York: Random House, 1983), 112.

5. See Christopher Green, *Negative Taxes and the Poverty Problem* (Washington, D.C.: The Brookings Institution, 1967) for technical analysis of these relationships.

6. See H. Richard Niebuhr, *Radical Monotheism and Western Culture* (New York: Harper & Brothers, 1960).

7. Edgar Sheffield Brightman, *An Introduction to Philosophy*, rev. ed. (New York: Henry Holt & Co., 1951), 140–41.

8. Stanley Hauerwas and James M. Gustafson, while not ignoring social issues, represent this emphasis on character as the decisive sphere of the moral life. See Stanley Hauerwas, *Character and the Christian Life: A Study in Theological Ethics* (San Antonio, Texas: Trinity Univ. Press, 1975) and James M. Gustafson, *Christ and the Moral Life* (New York: Harper & Row, 1969).

9. Conversations with white church leaders and teachers from South Africa in recent years do make it clear that a substantial part of the white population there does regard the apartheid system as a problem of tragic proportions. Whether they will persuade others to change in time to prevent further deterioration of an already chaotic social situation remains to be seen.

10. The monetary policies of the early 1980s in the United States were largely the responsibility of the independent (or quasi-independent) Federal Reserve Board, of course. However, both the White House and Fed applied the "hard medicine" with vigor during that period.

11. Thurow's *Zero-Sum Society,* again, reminds us of the competitive, conflictual realities at work in much economic life.

12. John C. Bennett, et al., *Christian Values and Economic Life* (New York: Harper & Brothers, 1954).

Chapter Two

1. Milton and Rose Friedman, *Free to Choose: A Personal Statement* (New York: Avon Books, 1980), 5.

2. Canaan Sodido Banana, *The Theology of Promise: The Dynamics of Self-Reliance* (Harare, Zimbabwe: College Press, 1982), 49–50.

3. World Council of Churches, *The Church and the Disorder of Society,* Amsterdam Assembly Series (New York: Harper & Brothers, 1948), 192.

4. Adam Smith, *An Inquiry Into the Nature and Causes of the Wealth of Nations* (1776), book 5, chap. 2.

5. See Milton Friedman, *Capitalism and Freedom* (Chicago: Univ. of Chicago Press, 1962); Milton and Rose Friedman, *Free to Choose: A Personal Statement* (New York: Avon Books, 1980); George Gilder, *Wealth and Poverty* (New York: Basic Books, 1981); Michael Novak, *The Spirit of Democratic Capitalism* (New York: Simon & Schuster, 1982).

6. This theme was especially prominent in the Friedmans' *Free to Choose* and the television series on which the book was partly based.

7. This theme is implicit throughout *The Spirit of Democratic Capitalism* and has been stated repeatedly in Novak's public lectures.

8. Gilder, *Wealth and Poverty,* 37–38.

9. Ibid., 262.

10. Ibid., 21–27.

11. John Locke, *Second Treatise on Civil Government* (1690).

12. Karl Polanyi, *The Great Transformation: The Political and Economic Origins of Our Time* (Boston: Beacon Press, 1957 [1944]).

13. Ibid., 78.

14. Ibid., 141.

15. Ibid., 150.

16. Gilder, *Wealth and Poverty,* 22.

17. See especially Ayn Rand, *The Virtue of Selfishness: A New Concept of Egoism* (New York: New American Library, 1964).

18. See Lester C. Thurow, *Dangerous Currents: The State of Economics* (New York: Random House, 1983), 173–215, for a perceptive account of why a purely economic "price auction" model cannot account for actual wages.

19. M. Friedman, *Capitalism and Freedom*, 22–34.

20. Paul A. Samuelson, *Economics*, 9th ed. (New York: McGraw-Hill, 1973), 475.

21. M. Friedman, *Capitalism and Freedom*, 22–34.

22. Andrew Carnegie, "Democracy and the Gospel of Wealth," *North American Review* 148 (June 1889): 653–64.

23. Michael Harrington, *Socialism* (New York: Bantam Books, 1973 [1972]), 185.

24. This idea is reiterated and enlarged by the recent call from the 1975 Nairobi Assembly of the WCC for a "just, participatory, and sustainable society." The ecumenical concept of social responsibility is elaborated in Walter G. Muelder, *Foundations of the Responsible Society* (New York and Nashville: Abingdon Press, 1959) and *Religion and Economic Responsibility* (New York: Charles Scribner's Sons, 1953). The emphasis on "sustainability" is elaborated by Robert L. Stivers, *The Sustainable Society: Ethics and Economic Growth* (Philadelphia: Westminster Press, 1976).

25. Novak, *Spirit of Democratic Capitalism*, 57.

Chapter Three

1. Substantial parts of this chapter originally appeared in my paper "Theological Perspective on Economics," which was prepared for an international symposium on Morality of the Market, sponsored by the Fraser Institute in Vancouver, British Columbia. That paper appears in Walter Block, Geoffrey Brennan, and Kenneth Elzinga, eds., *Morality of the Market: Religious and Economic Perspectives* (Vancouver, B.C.: The Fraser Institute, 1985). The repeated material is used here by kind permission of the Fraser Institute.

2. Walter Rauschenbusch, *Christianity and the Social Crisis* (New York: Macmillan Co., 1907), 90.

3. H. Richard Niebuhr, *Radical Monotheism and Western Culture* (New York: Harper & Brothers, 1960).

4. See Bruce C. Birch and Larry L. Rasmussen, *Bible and Ethics in the Christian Life* (Minneapolis: Augsburg Pub. House, 1976) for deeper probing of the meaning of such passages than one usually encounters.

5. See esp. Karl Barth, *Church Dogmatics*, 3/1 (Edinburgh: T. & T. Clark, 1958).

6. That question is posed provocatively in Robert L. Heilbroner, *An Inquiry into the Human Prospect* (New York: W.W. Norton, 1975), 169ff.

7. See esp. Reinhold Niebuhr, *The Nature and Destiny of Man* (New York: Charles Scribner's Sons, 1941), perhaps the best twentieth-century account of the meaning of original sin.

8. See *The Marx-Engels Reader*, 2d ed., ed. Robert C. Tucker (New York and London: W.W. Norton & Co., 1978), 66–128, and Eric Fromm, *Marx's Concept of Man* (New York: Frederick Ungar, 1961).

9. George Gilder, *Wealth and Poverty* (New York: Basic Books, 1981), 24–27.

10. Michael Novak, *Toward a Theology of the Corporation* (Washington D.C.: American Enterprise Institute, 1981), 33.

11. T. S. Eliot, "Choruses from 'The Rock'," from *Collected Poems 1909–1962* (New York: Harcourt, Brace & World, 1934).

12. This insight forms the heart of St. Augustine's contrast between the "City of God" and the "City of Earth," and it is noteworthy that he saw the earthly city of mutual self-love as containing the seeds of its own destruction. He understood that to be the reason for the disintegration of Rome, already discernible in his time.

13. I have elaborated this distinction more fully in Philip Wogaman, *Guaranteed Annual Income: The Moral Issues* (New York and Nashville: Abingdon Press, 1968), 71–73.

Chapter Four

1. *Statistical Abstract of the United States 1984* (Washington, D.C.: U.S. Government Printing Office, 1984), 855, from data supplied by the *Statistical Yearbook* and *Monthly Bulletin of Statistics* of the United Nations.

2. The World Bank, *World Development Report 1984* (New York: Oxford Univ. Press, 1984), 218–19.

3. *Statistical Abstract*, 1984, and Alice M. Rivlin, ed., *Economic Choices 1984* (Washington, D.C.: The Brookings Institution, 1984), 157–71.

4. The World Bank, *World Development Report 1984*, 218–19.

5. It is a mistake to consider these figures and percentages as precise. Data from deeply impoverished societies with high rates of illiteracy are often questionable, and it is difficult enough to assemble reliable data for highly sophisticated countries. Moreover, in the poorest countries, some kinds of economic goods and services never make it into the official statistics, and these are goods and services that to some extent mitigate the harshest levels of destitution and help explain why people are able to survive at all where the official income figures seem inconsistent with human survival. Still, the figures, while not precisely accurate, do portray the economic reality. There are vast gulfs between poor people, who constitute more than half the world's population, and prosperous people, who represent a much smaller number.

6. U.S. data are from *Statistical Abstract* volumes for 1972 and 1984. British data are from Willem H. Buiter and Marcus H. Miller, "Changing the Rules: Economic Consequences of the Thatcher Regime," in William C. Brainard and George L. Perry, eds., *Brookings Papers on Economic Activity 2, 1983* (Washington, D.C.: The Brookings Institution, 1984), 336. In the U.S. each percentage point adds more than 1 million unemployed people; in the U.K. it adds 240,000.

7. See, e.g., Robert Theobald, *Free Men and Free Markets* (Garden City, N.Y.: Doubleday Anchor Books, 1963, 1965) and *The Challenge of Abundance* (New York: Clarkson N. Potter, 1961).

8. *Statistical Abstract 1984*, 419–20.

9. *Statistical Abstract 1984*, 883.

10. Rivlin, *Economic Choices 1984*, 69.

11. Paul Ehrlich, *The Population Bomb* (New York: Ballantine Books, 1968).

12. Donella H. Meadows, et al., *The Limits to Growth* (New York: Universe Books, 1972).

13. Jeremy Rifkin, *Entropy: A New World View* (New York: Viking Press, 1980).

14. Heilbroner anticipates the possibility of an era of authoritarian regimes in

many Third World settings since only such governments are likely to prove strong enough to deal with the objective economic and environmental problems there in the next decades.

15. See, e.g., the Worldwatch Paper series, with such titles as Erik P. Eckholm, *The Other Energy Crisis: Firewood* (no. 1, September 1975); Lester R. Brown, *The Politics and Responsibility of the North American Breadbasket* (no. 2, October 1975); Denis Hayes, *Energy: The Case for Conservation* (no. 4, January 1976); Denis Hayes, *Nuclear Power: The Fifth Horseman* (no. 6, May 1976); Patricia L. McGrath, *The Unfinished Assignment: Equal Education for Women* (no. 7, July 1976); Erik Eckholm and Lester R. Brown, *Spreading Deserts—The Hand of Man* (no. 13, August 1977); and Kathleen Newland, *Women and Population Growth: Choice Beyond Childbearing* (no. 16, December 1977). See also Erik P. Eckholm, *Losing Ground: Environmental Stress and World Food Prospects* (New York: W. W. Norton, 1976) and Lester R. Brown, *In The Human Interest* (New York: W. W. Norton, 1974).

16. Milton and Rose Friedman, *Free to Choose: A Personal Statement* (New York: Avon Books, 1980), 208.

Chapter Five

1. Robert Benne, *The Ethics of Democratic Capitalism: A Moral Reassessment* (Philadelphia: Fortress Press, 1981).

2. Michael Harrington, *Socialism* (New York: Bantam Books, 1973 [1972]), 11, 30.

3. Joseph A. Schumpeter, *Capitalism, Socialism and Democracy,* 3d ed. (New York: Harper & Row, 1950, 1962), 67.

4. Harrington, *Socialism,* 377.

5. I participated on the same program in the state of Kansas with one such an individual, whose theme was that even agricultural production was inevitably threatening to the long-run environmental future. In his opinion we should aim toward a return to a purely hunting and gathering economy for a world population reduced, ultimately, to 100 million persons!

6. *Statistical Abstract of the United States 1984* (Washington, D.C.: U.S. Government Printing Office, 1984), 865.

7. The Brandt Commission Report of 1980 has questioned the implicit paternalism in such IMF policies, noting that over the long run the debt-repayment record of Third World countries has been rather good. Willy Brandt, et al., *North–South: A Program for Survival* (Cambridge, Mass.: MIT Press, 1980), 215–17.

8. A lexical order is one in which the second item in a series is conditional on the first, the third on the second, and so on. We cannot assume that production is the first item in such a series without knowing more about the series. *Some* economic production is surely necessary to everything else, of course; but beyond a certain point production may compete with other priorities of greater ethical importance.

Chapter Six

1. Charles Murray, *Losing Ground: American Social Policy 1950–1980* (New York: Basic Books, 1984), 234.

2. Michael Harrington, *The Other America: Poverty in the United States* (New York: Macmillan Co., 1962), 10.

3. George Gilder, *Wealth and Poverty* (New York: Basic Books, 1981), 118.

4. John Rawls, *A Theory of Justice* (Cambridge, Mass.: Harvard Univ. Press, 1971), 15.

5. Arthur M. Okun, *Equality and Efficiency: The Big Tradeoff* (Washington, D.C.: The Brookings Institution, 1975).

6. Ibid., 64

7. Fred Hirsch, *Social Limits to Growth* (Cambridge, Mass.: Harvard Univ. Press, 1976), 27ff.

8. There were, in 1960, nearly 40 million Americans below the poverty line. That number decreased to 33.2 million in 1965 and to 25.4 million in 1968. It remained at or below that level until 1980, when it increased to 29.3 million, and 1982, when it was up to 34.4 million: *Statistical Abstract of the United States 1984* (Washington, D.C.: U.S. Government Printing Office, 1984), 471. The U.S. Bureau of the Census reports figures in the 34 to 35 million range for 1984, decreasing to 33.7 million in 1985. There is some debate over the effect of in-kind welfare programs such as Medicaid, food stamps, and housing subsidies on the numbers of people below the poverty line. Since these programs cannot easily be factored into calculations of poverty status (particularly the programs that are available to or used by a minority of poor people—such as housing subsidies and Medicaid), we can assume that the current numbers of poor people are somewhat less than the given statistics. There is little doubt, however, that the number remains large and that it has in fact increased since the 1960s.

9. Gilder, *Wealth and Poverty,* 117.

10. See especially chaps. 4, 11, and 14.

11. Murray argues that social reformers have done the poor (and especially blacks) a disservice by identifying the "system," or social circumstances beyond their control, as responsible for their plight. The inevitable effect of this is, in his judgment, the misdirection of anger and the development of a kind of passive dependency among poor people. There may be some truth to that, as Jesse Jackson and other reform advocates acknowledge. And poor people facing even the worst circumstances can usually improve their situations by hard work. Nevertheless, Murray devotes scant attention to the extent to which problems *are* systemic and to the fact that conservative political leadership scuttled the Community Action Program when it appeared to have aroused too much activism among poor people.

12. Phillip Keisling, "Lessons of the Great Society," *The Washington Monthly* (December 1984): 51–52.

13. Robert J. Samuelson, "Escaping the Poverty Trap," *Newsweek* (September 10, 1984): 60.

14. See Christopher Green, *Negative Taxes and the Poverty Problem* (Washington, D.C.: The Brookings Institution, 1967); Philip Wogaman, *Guaranteed Annual Income: The Moral Issues* (New York and Nashville: Abingdon Press, 1968); Milton Friedman, *Capitalism and Freedom* (Chicago: Univ. of Chicago Press, 1962); Daniel P. Moynihan, *The Politics of A Guaranteed Income: The Nixon Administration and the Family Assistance Plan* (New York: Random House, 1973). In the wake of experiments with the negative income tax in several states in the 1970s, there is general recognition that an income guarantee will have some (though not necessarily much) negative effect on work incentives. Note, for exam-

ple, Robert A. Moffit, "The Negative Income Tax: Would It Discourage Work?" in *Monthly Labor Review* 104 (April 1981): 23–27. Sar A. Levitan and Clifford M. Johnson provide an important cautionary note, however, in their *Beyond the Safety Net: Reviving the Promise of Opportunity in America* (Cambridge, Mass.: Ballinger Pub. Co., 1984): "Given the absence of opportunities and the limited rewards for work when jobs are available, it is perhaps surprising that the poor have not responded to subsistence benefits and high marginal tax rates by dropping out of the labor force in far greater numbers. Research findings suggest that when welfare recipients are faced with benefit reduction rates of less than 100 percent, their work effort is affected only moderately by variations in benefit levels and marginal tax rates" (p. 107).

  15. Ronald Pasquariello, *Tax Justice: Social and Moral Aspects of American Tax Policy* (Lanham, Md., London, and New York: Univ. Press of America, 1985), 59. See also Henry J. Aaron and Harvey Galper, *Assessing Tax Reform* (Washington, D.C.: The Brookings Institution, 1985) and Joseph A. Pechman, *Who Paid the Taxes, 1966–85* (Washington, D.C.: The Brookings Institution, 1985). Pechman concluded that the total tax burden in the United States was more regressive in 1985 than 1966, partly because of the rise in payroll tax rates and partly because of reductions in corporate income and property taxes.

Chapter Seven

1. Michael D. Reagan, "For a Guaranteed Income," *The New York Times Magazine* (June 7, 1964).

2. *Pastoral Letter on Catholic Social Teaching and the U.S. Economy. Origins* (Washington, D.C.: U.S. Catholic Conference, Nov. 15, 1984), 359.

3. M. Harvey Brenner, *Estimating the Social Cost of National Economic Policy* (Washington, D.C.: U.S. Congress, Joint Economic Committee, 1976).

4. David Owen, *A Future That Will Work* (Harmondsworth, England: Penguin Books, 1984), 97.

5. Sar A. Levitan and Clifford M. Johnson, *Beyond the Safety Net: Reviving the Promise of Opportunity in America* (Cambridge, Mass.: Ballinger Pub. Co., 1984), 38–41.

6. Martin Anderson, *Welfare* (Stanford, Calif.: Hoover Institution Press, 1978), 162. Quoted by Levitan and Johnson, *Beyond the Safety Net*, 29.

7. Levitan and Johnson, *Beyond the Safety Net*, 38.

8. Source: U.S. Bureau of Labor Statistics.

9. *Statistical Abstract of the United States 1984* (Washington, D.C.: U.S. Government Printing Office, 1984), 140–41.

10. Milton Friedman, *Capitalism and Freedom* (Chicago: Univ. of Chicago Press, 1962), 89. The proposal is also endorsed by Charles Murray, *Losing Ground: American Social Policy 1950–1980* (New York: Basic Books, 1984), 224.

11. Both Friedman and Murray appear to be impressed by the attractions of private school education, based on what they perceive to be the higher quality of its product, and the voucher scheme is partly designed to open this option to the general run of the population. We may note, however, two elements in private school education that help account for its quality in those schools that are, in fact, superior to public schools in America: first, that it can be selective in its admissions policies—and there is nothing like a good student body to guarantee good

graduates—and second, that it enjoys a favorable faculty-to-student ratio. Neither of these points is spoken to directly by the proposed voucher system. If, armed with their governmental educational vouchers, parents could claim equal access to all private schools (the latter being forced to adopt open admissions policies like most public schools), that might lower the quality of those schools. But if parents could not claim that right, of what value would the vouchers be in improving their children's education? And if, flooded with vast numbers of new students, the private schools (or reconstituted public schools) could maintain the favorable teacher-to-student ratio, they could do so only at much greater cost. Why not solve the problem directly by improving the pupil–teacher ratio in the existing public school system?

12. See John R. Silber, "Tuition Advance Fund," in *Vital Speeches* 44 (January 15, 1978): 214–18, and "Tuition Dilemma: A New Way to Pay the Bills," in *The Atlantic Monthly* 242: 1 (July 1978): 31–32, 33–36. Silber's proposal would require a substantial public outlay to establish the fund; thereafter it would, as a social investment, be self-financing.

13. Dean M. Kelley, *Why Churches Should Not Pay Taxes* (New York: Harper & Row, 1977).

Chapter Eight

1. See, e.g., Lynn White, Jr., "The Historical Roots of Our Ecologic Crisis," *Science* 155: 3767 (March 10, 1967): 1203–7; Frederick Elder, *Crisis in Eden: A Religious Study of Man and Environment* (New York and Nashville: Abingdon Press, 1970); Robert L. Stivers, *The Sustainable Society: Ethics and Economic Growth* (Philadelphia: Westminster Press, 1976); John Cobb, "Ecology, Ethics, and Theology," in Herman E. Daly, ed., *Toward a Steady-State Economy* (San Francisco: W. H. Freeman and Co., 1973); James C. Logan, "Ecological Considerations," in J. Philip Wogaman, ed., *The Population Crisis and Moral Responsibility* (Washingtong, D.C.: Public Affairs Press, 1973), 95–108.

2. Since Nairobi, the ecumenical discussion in World Council circles has emphasized the quest for a society that is "just, participatory, and sustainable," each of the three being considered essential to the other two.

3. See Robert Heilbroner, *An Inquiry into the Human Prospect* (New York: W. W. Norton, 1975), 169–76.

4. Milton and Rose Friedman, *Free to Choose: A Personal Statement* (New York: Avon Books, 1980), 206.

5. Milton Friedman, *Capitalism and Freedom* (Chicago: Univ. of Chicago Press, 1962), 27–32.

6. Friedman and Friedman, *Free to Choose,* 203–8.

7. See, e.g., George Gilder, *Wealth and Poverty* (New York: Basic Books, 1981), 255.

8. Erik P. Eckholm, *Losing Ground: Environmental Stress and World Food Prospects* (New York: W. W. Norton, 1976), 25–45; Lester J. Bilsky, ed., *Historical Ecology: Essays on Environment and Social Change* (Port Washington, N.Y., and London: Kennikat Press, 1980); J. Donald Hughes, *Ecology in Ancient Civilizations* (Albuquerque: Univ. of New Mexico Press, 1975).

9. Frank Feather, ed., *Through the '80s: Thinking Globally, Acting Locally* (Washington, D.C.: World Future Society, 1980).

10. Carl Sagan has issued a warning about the grave potential dangers in our continued reliance on use of fossil fuels through creation of a "greenhouse effect" that raises average world temperatures a few degrees, melting polar ice and raising sea levels enough to flood coastal cities, etc. See Carl Sagan, "The Warming of the World," *Parade* (February 3, 1985). Others, by contrast, have warned of a new ice age. Plainly, scientists must engage in much conjecture about the long-run effects of major environmental intrusions. But that is exactly my point. In the absence of hard data about fundamentally important things, a certain caution is in order.

11. I am thinking in particular of the, to me, misguided views of a number of the socialist-bloc representatives at the World Population Conference in 1974 who treated runaway population growth rates as a matter of no concern and who bitterly criticized the "neo-Malthusians" of the West for using the population-explosion specter to avoid their own exploitative imperialism. One of these countries was China, which in the decade since 1974 has had to impose very draconian policies on its people to curb what the Chinese now recognize to be ruinous population growth in the world's largest country. By the second World Population Conference in Mexico City, in 1984, roles had largely reversed and a U.S. administration committed to laissez-faire took a complacent attitude toward population growth rates.

Chapter Nine

1. Willy Brandt, in *North–South, A Program for Survival* (Cambridge, Mass.: MIT Press, 1980), 13.

2. Pope John XXIII, "Pacem in Terris," in *Seven Great Encyclicals* (Glen Rock, N.J.: Paulist Press, 1963), par. 131, p. 316.

3. See Reinhold Niebuhr, *Moral Man and Immoral Society* (New York: Charles Scribner's Sons, 1932) for a still-timely analysis of how individuals can use group loyalties as a way of enhancing self-interest.

4. James H. Weaver and Marguerite Berger, "The Marxist Critique of Dependency Theory: An Introduction," in Charles K. Wilber, ed., *The Political Economy of Development and Underdevelopment*, 3d ed. (New York: Random House, 1983), 61.

5. Bruce C. Birch and Larry L. Rasmussen, *The Predicament of the Prosperous* (Philadelphia: Westminster Press, 1978).

6. See André Gunder Frank, "The Development of Underdevelopment," in Wilber, *Development and Underdevelopment*, 99–108, and Celso Furtado, *Economic Development of Latin America: A Survey from Colonial Times to the Cuban Revolution* (Cambridge: Cambridge Univ. Press, 1970), for classic statements of the theory.

7. The World Bank, *World Development Report 1984* (New York: Oxford Univ. Press, 1984), 31.

8. W. Arthur Lewis has made a number of valuable suggestions in his *Evolution of the International Economic Order* (Princeton: Princeton Univ. Press, 1978).

9. See, e.g., Richard J. Barnet and Ronald E. Muller, *Global Reach: The Power of the Multinational Corporations* (New York: Simon & Schuster, 1974); Nasrollah S. Fatemi and Gail W. Williams, *Multinational Corporations* (Cran-

bury, N.J.: A. S. Barnes, 1975); Jack N. Behrman, "Codes for Transnational Enterprises," in Ivan Hill, ed., *The Ethical Basis of Economic Freedom* (New York: Praeger Publishers, 1980), 125–58.

10. See Weaver and Berger, "Marxist Critique."

11. Unfortunately, the staff of the World Health Organization itself did not interpret and implement the code vigorously, thereby making it easier for less scrupulous companies to take advantage of Nestlé's code compliance in a number of Third World markets. The code, as a precedent, was thereby weakened to some extent. But it still stands as a most interesting and, in the main, effective new kind of venture by the international community.

12. Estimates of the number of people who have died in small wars, revolutions, etc., since the end of World War II vary from 10 to 25 million. The wars include the Korean conflict, the Vietnam War, the various Arab-Israeli wars, the Iran-Iraq war, revolutions throughout Africa and Latin America, the struggle over Kampuchea, and a host of others. Some who have likened this period to the nineteenth-century era of peace are plainly off the mark, although the major powers have at least avoided direct military engagement with each other.

13. World Bank, *World Development Report 1984*, 150.

14. Brandt et al, *North-South*, 14.

Chapter Ten

1. Herman Wouk, *The Caine Mutiny* (New York: Doubleday & Co., 1951), 59–62.

2. Sar A. Levitan and Clifford M. Johnson, *Beyond the Safety Net: Reviving the Promise of Opportunity in America* (Cambridge, Mass.: Ballinger Pub. Co., 1984), 42.

Index